Dear Mr. & Mrs Golangco,

Hope you had
down under!

Here's a little keepsake to
remind you of all the
wonderful food Melbourne
has to offer!!

Lotsa love,
Al & Mad's friends!

THE GREAT
Aussie
Barbie
COOKBOOK

Kim Terakes

Photography by Rob Palmer

VIKING
an imprint of
PENGUIN BOOKS

VIKING

Published by the Penguin Group
Penguin Group (Australia)
250 Camberwell Road, Camberwell, Victoria 3124, Australia
(a division of Pearson Australia Group Pty Ltd)
Penguin Group (USA) Inc.
375 Hudson Street, New York, New York 10014, USA
Penguin Group (Canada)
90 Eglinton Avenue East, Suite 700, Toronto, Canada ON M4P 2Y3
(a division of Pearson Penguin Canada Inc.)
Penguin Books Ltd
80 Strand, London WC2R 0RL England
Penguin Ireland
25 St Stephen's Green, Dublin 2, Ireland
(a division of Penguin Books Ltd)
Penguin Books India Pvt Ltd
11 Community Centre, Panchsheel Park, New Delhi – 110 017, India
Penguin Group (NZ)
67 Apollo Drive, Rosedale, North Shore 0632, New Zealand
(a division of Pearson New Zealand Ltd)
Penguin Books (South Africa) (Pty) Ltd
24 Sturdee Avenue, Rosebank, Johannesburg 2196, South Africa

Penguin Books Ltd, Registered Offices: 80 Strand, London, WC2R 0RL, England

First published by Penguin Group (Australia), 2007

10 9 8 7 6 5

Text copyright © Kim Terakes 2007
Photographs copyright © Rob Palmer 2007

Designed by Daniel New © Penguin Group (Australia)
Cover and author photographs by Rob Palmer
Styling by David Morgan
Typeset in Clarendon and ITC Franklin Gothic by Post Pre-press Group,
Brisbane, Queensland
Colour reproduction by Splitting Image, Clayton, Victoria
Printed and bound in China by 1010 Printing International Limited

National Library of Australia
Cataloguing-in-Publication data:

Terakes, Kim.
    The great Aussie barbie cookbook.

    Includes index.
    ISBN 978 0 670 07147 0 (pbk.).

    1. Barbecue cookery. I. Title.

641.5784

penguin.com.au

Contents

The Great Aussie Barbie

The Great Aussie Barbie has come a long way. In the 1960s, when I was a kid, barbecuing had really taken hold in the suburbs of Australia. We embraced this nouveau way of entertaining with gusto, as it was so well suited to our climate and laid-back sensibilities. Cooking? Outside? No cleaning up? You beauty!

Barbecuing allowed blokes to take credit for doing very little. While the women did the shopping, cleaned the house, made the starters, the salads and desserts and cleaned up afterwards, all the bloke did was burn the steaks and bangers – but *HE WAS COOKING*.

The barbecue itself was still less than sophisticated though. It was usually just a few sheets of iron balanced on some old housebricks (though if you were posh you had a proper brick one). From there we graduated to those fragile-looking portable things, with three ready-to-snap aluminium legs as thick as tinfoil. Then along came the kettle barbecue, which soon became incredibly popular, with a devoted bunch of followers who cooked everything from whole legs of lamb to pavs on them.

Next we marvelled at the advent of Heat Beads to replace humble charcoal, which gave a more even cooking temperature and meant we didn't burn our chops as often. These could be lit with the help of those noxious white firelighters (I don't know whether it's the smell of the horrible white cubes that permeates the food, or whether it just stays up your nostrils for days, but everything ends up tasting of them).

And then came the high-tech gas barbecues that were the forerunners of what most Australians use today. They started off as fairly spartan pieces of equipment, with just two burners, a flat grillplate and a chargrill. Now you can get barbies so large you virtually need planning permission for them, and they have all sorts of attachments and doovers to play with – wok burners, baking dishes, rotisseries, and lids that turn the barbie into an oven.

As for tomorrow? Well, I've seen some plans for next-generation barbecues and they're James Bond-meets-the-Jetsons. As well as cooking innovations like built-in smokers, teppanyaki plates and double woks, there'll be all sorts of unexpected features, including audio speakers, 'mood' lighting and even flash corkscrews, as manufacturers try to out-accessorise each other. Your barbecue could easily end up being four or five metres long.

Barbecuing is as popular today as it has ever been, but what we cook on the barbie is changing. We Aussies have always thought of ourselves as world champion barbecuers, but in reality things were just burnt steaks and bangers for a long time. We've since smartened up our ideas a bit, and are starting to realise that good food cooked well on the barbie is one of the great joys of life.

We're expanding our repertoire of recipes to reflect the multicultural society in which we live. Walk into a food court in any suburban shopping centre and you'll have a choice of Indian, Chinese, Japanese, Vietnamese, Malaysian, Thai, Italian, Lebanese, Mexican and Australian/English/ American food, just for starters. The wide array of flavours now available has changed the Australian palate, so much so that we will no longer settle for the boring, bland, grey English food that our parents and grandparents endured, and especially not on the barbecue. We want big, vibrant, clean flavours, particularly from Asia and the Mediterranean, and that is what you will find in this book.

I run regular barbecue cooking classes (see aussiebarbie.com.au), and I've found the expectations of the students (mostly guys) are pretty straightforward:

- they want to know how to cook your basic steaks and bangers better;

- they want to learn a few barbie trade secrets;

- and most important of all, they want a couple of reliable dishes that are a bit different, that they can whip up to impress their mates (they don't want fifty, just one or two will do, but they must be good).

Accordingly, the recipes in this book cover the basics and a bit more. They dart proudly from traditional (lamb cutlets), to stylish (milk-fed veal), to abject dagginess (The Great Aussie Steak Sambo), and back again. Some dishes would look quite at home in a swish restaurant, while others should never be let out of the backyard. Crucially, though, I stick to things that belong on a barbecue because they work on a barbecue – no tricky-dick stuff just for the sake of it. You could probably cook a soufflé on one of those new-generation barbecues, but why would you want to?

The same principles apply to barbecuing as any other sort of cooking: just buy the best quality fresh produce you can get, and don't mess with it. You won't believe the difference cooking food simply and following a few basic golden rules makes to the end result.

Finally, the most important thing is to relax and enjoy cooking on your barbecue, because we all know that an Aussie barbie is about much more than just food cooked on a grill. It's about spending time with your family and friends, sharing food and conversation, having a few beers with your mates. It's backyard cricket, blockout lotion and mozzie spray. It's noisy kids in the pool, long afternoon naps and soggy paper plates.

It's the heart and soul of Australian life.

Hints & tips

Tools of the trade

If you're one of those industrious types that like a challenge, the good news is that you can barbecue on just about anything. Give a man a piece of metal and a few house bricks, and barbecue he will. There are all sorts of contraptions I've seen people use over the years (one fashioned from an old shopping trolley springs to mind), and although each of these had varying degrees of success in cooking food to a standard fit for consumption, they sum up the 'have a go' attitude of the Aussie barbie.

But for those of you who feel more comfortable cooking with equipment specifically built for the job, here's the lowdown on what's available.

Gas barbecues

The vast majority of barbecues used in Australia are gas-powered, so let's cover those first. Your standard version will have a basic flat grillplate and chargrill, perfect for any sort of grilling, which is all that most people want to do on the barbie. Some models include a baking dish with a lid and an extra gas burner for slow-cooking (so you can have a flame either side of the dish but not directly underneath it). Others come with a wok burner at one end on which you can stir-fry or cook in a saucepan. This effectively means you can use your barbecue as your kitchen stove, with the added bonus of being outdoors, so you can go ahead and cook those messy, smelly dishes that can be so unpopular in the kitchen. Your more upmarket gas barbecue may include a rotisserie, but these are a bit like the breadmaker/ice cream machine/crêpemaker – they're a nice novelty but they usually end up residing in the back of the cupboard before too long.

These extra features make the humble barbie so versatile that you can use it to cook almost any meal. Now that more and more people are converted to the pleasures of cooking and eating outside, some even get their barbies built in to their outdoor dining area, with gas connected through the mains.

Barbecues not powered by gas

(This includes kettle barbecues, wood-fired barbecues, and the like.)

Using a charcoal or wood-fired barbecue requires more skill and patience than cooking with gas, as you have to wait for the flames to die down so the coals are at just the right temperature. While the results can be terrific, it's a trade-off between the instant gratification of gas (perfect for busy weeknights) and the slow-burn, more hands-on and possibly more rewarding process of using wood or charcoal (nice for special occasions).

There's a huge variety of charcoal and wood-fired barbecues available, including smaller versions for use on apartment balconies, and even portable versions to take to the beach or park.

Slow-cooking on charcoal or wood-fired barbies is possible, but is more complex than with the gas equivalent. It takes plenty of practice, as you need to be able to control the heat to maintain a constant temperature over a long period. It's perfect for those who like a challenge, and the results can be very satisfying, but if you take your eye off the ball after one too many beers, you're in trouble.

Other stuff

There's a host of barbecue accessories on the market, most of which you won't ever need. For example, a set of grossly oversized, probably-bright-red-handled barbecue tools are right up there in the pointless and daggy stakes (but they do go nicely with the 'boobs' apron you got last Christmas). What is it about cooking outdoors that compels us blokes to use implements three times the normal size? If you're not even going to prick the sausages (which you shouldn't, because all the natural juices will run out and the fat will burn), why do you need a fork big enough for the devil to wield? Maybe they're useful for turning large lumps of meat like legs of lamb, but that's about all.

A pair of long-handled tongs is your most indispensable barbecue tool, and these are really important so that your 'turning' hand doesn't end up medium-rare.

You can buy barbecue spatulas that double as scrapers to clean your hotplate, and sometimes even have a sharp edge to act as a (rather cumbersome) knife as well. These are handy for turning delicate fish that could break up with tongs, and useful for cleaning, but buy a good quality knife for cutting. A clean paint scraper is also really handy for cleaning the barbecue plate.

Be prepared

Believe it or not, a little bit of preparation goes a long way.

The art of the shopping list

First off you'll need a shopping list – it's really boring having to run back to the shops to get the one thing you forgot, or spending hours wandering about because you can't remember what you came for. Instead of the usual stream-of-consciousness list that most of us make, with no order or logical sequence to the items, try this. Make six columns on a page: one for fruit and veg, one for the butcher, one for seafood, one for the deli, one for supermarket stuff, and one for your cup-boards at home to check that you have what you think you have. Then go through each recipe and write the ingredients in the appropriate columns. Tick off the items you already have in the cupboard, and go forth and shop! This list takes no more time than an ordinary list, and makes shopping a hell of a lot more efficient.

Timing is everything

It's a barbecue and you don't want to get too serious about things, but a little forward planning can make your barbie much more successful. Think about how long it will take to cook the steaks, allowing time for the meat to rest after cooking, then work backwards so you know when to start the vegetables. Spuds will need quite a while, but snow peas take thirty seconds to cook, so they should be heading for the boiling water around the same time as the steaks are being put on plates.

Also, if you're having a few friends over, think about the plates and platters you will need. It's a lot easier finding them and getting them out beforehand than rummaging around in the cupboards while your hungry guests watch the food go cold.

Get meat in the mood

All meat, poultry and seafood should be at room temperature when you cook it, so it cooks more evenly. If it's cold when you throw it on the barbie, the outside will cook quickly, but the inside will take much longer.

Take it out of the fridge half an hour or so before you cook it (but keep it covered and don't leave it in blazing sunlight – food poisoning is *so* overrated).

Cut the food, not your fingers

Not all of us have the deft chopping skills of professional chefs, but that doesn't stop us having a red-hot go. Here's a tip to help you keep all your fingers intact: instead of holding the food with your fingers extended, bend them at the last knuckle and run the blade of the knife alongside the middle section of your fingers – that way you might still have a career as a concert pianist ahead of you.

No bouncy bouncy

If you are doing a fair bit of slicing and chopping, put a folded tea towel under your chopping board so you don't have two hard surfaces bouncing against each other. It's such a small thing, but you will really notice the difference.

Wok full of trouble

If you're using a wok, note that they work best over a very high heat with not too much food in them. Stir-frying is just that – frying. If you put too much food in a wok, you will be stewing the food rather than frying it. So if you have a lot to cook, do it in small batches.

Remember the golden rule – same size, same cooking time – if you are cooking an assortment of meat and vegies in your wok. Make sure you cut them all the same size so they take roughly the same amount of time to cook. Harder vegetables like carrots may need blanching first as they can take a lot longer to cook.

Teach the satay sticks to swim

Satay sticks are made from wood, right? And wood, especially skinny little bits of wood, burn, right? That's why you have to soak wooden or bamboo skewers in water for an hour before you thread the food on and throw them on the grill. They're still made out of wood and they'll still burn, but it will take a lot longer.

There's nothing like having a spare

Even with the convenience of swap-able gas bottles, there's nothing more inconvenient than running out of gas when the steaks are half-cooked. For the relatively small amount it costs, buying a second gas cylinder to have in reserve makes plenty of sense. That way you always have a full one on hand – assuming of course that you remember to swap the spare when it's empty.

Making the most of your barbie

It's easy to turn an ordinary meal on the barbie into something special, even on a school night.

Chicken, fish and vegies

Chicken works a treat on the barbie, but you need to cook it over a moderate heat so the outside doesn't burn before the insides are done. Or you can bake chicken by turning the heat off from directly below the meat and using the burners on either side, then closing the hood. This is a great way to cook chicken evenly and prevents it drying out. It is really important that you cook chicken thoroughly all the way through – test this by inserting a skewer or the point of a sharp knife into the thickest part. If the juices are clear, it's cooked; if they're pink or bloody, it needs more time.

The best fish for the barbie are the more dense, meatier fish like tuna or swordfish, or thick white fish like blue eye. Oily fish such as mackerel are good too, as they won't dry out. Delicate fish like snapper will fare better cooked in a parcel (see below).

The flavour of chargrilled vegetables is hard to beat, and most veggies (though possibly not peas) work well on the grill. Just remember that hard vegetables like potatoes, pumpkin or sweet potato need to be sliced no thicker than about 0.5 cm to cook through on the grill without burning. Asparagus, zucchini, capsicums and red onion are particularly good cooked on the barbie, the last three being perfect on a veggie kebab.

All wrapped up

Some foods, like delicate fish, really benefit from being cooked wrapped in a parcel of foil, or more exotic wrapping such as banana or pandan leaves. This will protect the food from the direct heat of the barbecue and contact with the grillplate, which means your fish won't break up when you cook it. You can add all sorts of flavourings to the parcel (herbs, spices or oils) to infuse the fish with flavour. Just remember, though, the parcel is sealed, which means the food will steam rather than grill, which is no bad thing, but don't expect a charred, caramelised skin when you unwrap your parcel.

Go low to cook slow

Barbecues are getting bigger and better all the time, which means we can do much more interesting things on them than just frying and grilling – like slow cooking. The only way to slow cook on a barbie is to have heat on both sides of the food and none directly under it – with the hood closed, of course. No matter how low you turn the heat, a gas barbecue will burn the bum out of your food every time if it cooks directly above the gas jets.

Here's the rub

Spice rubs and marinades are a great way to add flavour to meat, fish or even vegetables cooked on the barbie, and they give you the opportunity to seriously show off by creating your own unique combinations of flavours. Take the time to experiment first though, before you unleash a new 'taste' on your unsuspecting guests – some combinations work better than others.

A spice rub is a blend of dried spices that forms a tasty crust on barbecued food. You can buy spice rubs ready-made by the likes of MasterFoods – think Moroccan or Cajun, for starters – or you can mix up your own based on the distinctive flavours of a national cuisine (for example, combine ground cumin, coriander and turmeric for a taste of India).

There are plenty of ideas for marinades in this book, but it's really easy to create your own. Olive oil usually plays a part, to which you can add any combination of flavours: red or white wine, lemon or lime juice, vinegars, soy sauce, garlic, ginger, honey, or all sorts of fresh and dried herbs. For an Asian influence, try adding lemongrass, kaffir lime leaves, red shallots and chillies to ginger, garlic and fish sauce. Just tread carefully when using acidulants like vinegar and lime or lemon juice – these tend to 'cook' the fish or meat, so use them sparingly.

Marinades can really add zing to barbecued food, but a little restraint is sometimes required. A thin slice of veal or beef doesn't need to swim in a strongly flavoured marinade for 24 hours, whereas a large leg of lamb could take that sort of treatment.

Taking stock

Most stock cubes are nasty little things that are full of chemicals and have nothing to do with real food. Look instead for packs of ready-made liquid stock (in Tetra Paks) in your supermarket, which are the next step up in quality and taste. This stock is fine for general use in dishes like paella, risotto and noodles, but will need diluting with an equal amount of water first.

Homemade stock tastes best of all, and making chicken stock is a breeze and will earn you plenty of kudos amongst your mates. There are lots of complicated recipes out there, but all you really need for a basic chicken stock is a whole chook or 1 kg chicken bones, and some salt and pepper. Feel free to add any spare veg you might have lurking in the bottom of the fridge (onions, carrots, celery etc.) and some herbs if you like. Throw all this into a large pan of water, bring to the boil, then simmer for an hour, and it's done. Strain off the solids, and you're ready to go.

Fish stock is just as easy and even quicker. Use the bones from a white-fleshed fish, plus a little carrot, celery and onion and maybe a few black peppercorns and parsley stalks. Add to a large pan of water and simmer (half an hour should be plenty).

Beef or veal stock can be a real bugger to make (what with roasting the meat first and literally days spent simmering and skimming), so these are best left to the experts. Buy this ready-made if you need it.

The good oil

Here's the essential on oils, and everything you need to know about making a great salad, every time.

Bland is (very occasionally) best

You'll see the term 'neutral oil' used throughout the book. It's by no means a universal term, but it's one I use as shorthand for any oil that is good for grilling and frying, as it has a high smoking temperature and doesn't have a strong flavour to impart to food. This means you can safely rub it all over food or the grillplate before cooking and it won't intrude on the flavour of the dish. Good examples of neutral oils are peanut oil, vegetable oil, safflower oil and canola oil. (Some peanut oils from Asian food stores can have a stronger taste, so stick to a milder one bought from your supermarket.)

Steer well clear of palm oil, which is a highly saturated fat (seriously not good for you), and good old dripping (rendered meat fat) because, although it adds miles of flavour, it's not really a healthy option.

Olive oils ain't always olive oils

Olive oil is a pretty confusing subject. It's not easy to find really good ones and there is a lot of misinformation out there, as well as some dodgy labelling. We don't have the same quality standards as Europe, so we often get European rejects dumped here (including olive oils that aren't even made from olives), so watch out!

Your best bet is to buy olive oil from a specialty store, where you can taste the oil before you buy it, rather than from a supermarket. Good olive oil should taste clean and slightly peppery (and should smell like a fruit shop). Trust your own palate and buy what appeals to you. Try to find young oils – old is bad, as is light and heat, so avoid buying oil in clear bottles, and make sure you store your oil in a cool, dark spot.

Olive oil is generally not recommended for frying – good ones are relatively expensive and so are better saved for salads, where the flavour of the oil is really crucial, or to brush over meat or fish before grilling. I recommend buying extra virgin olive oil if you can: you'll really taste the difference.

Idiot-proof salad dressing

There are a million variations on a good salad dressing of course, but as long as you remember the following basic ratio of oil and vinegar, you can't go wrong. Remember – the better the quality of the oil and vinegar you use, the better the dressing will taste.

2 parts oil
1 part vinegar, lemon or lime juice
sea salt and freshly ground black pepper

You can experiment with all sorts of oils: a good quality extra virgin olive oil is most popular, and you can try varieties from Italy, Spain, Greece and of course now Australia. You can also try walnut oil or hazelnut oil as a nice alternative. The same goes for vinegar: balsamic, red wine or white wine are equally good.

For a change, try adding some other flavours to the dressing, such as a little mustard (grain or Dijon). This is standard practice for some people, and others I know always add sugar, for reasons best known to themselves. You can add a crushed clove of garlic or, for a more subtle garlic flavour, rub a cut clove around your salad bowl to 'scent' it. Add plenty of finely chopped fresh herbs to give any dressing a lift.

Make salads the last things you make

Some people make their salads hours before they're going to be eaten. Crazy when you think about it, as who wants limp and soggy lettuce? Wash and dry your leaves and keep them in a plastic bag in the fridge. When you're ready to eat, mix the dressing in your salad bowl, then toss the salad through the dressing just before you serve it so the leaves stay nice and crisp.

How to cook the perfect steak

This book is all about giving you ideas beyond your basic steaks and bangers on the barbie. However, there's no denying that the quintessential Australian barbecue dish is the perfectly cooked steak, so not only do you need to know how to do it, you need to know how to do it well.

Here's what NOT to do:

✘ Buy any old piece of meat because it's 'only a barbecue'.

✘ Turn the barbecue on and hope that the heat will kill the germs in the layer of debris still there from the last time you used it.

✘ Pour plenty of oil all over the hotplate.

✘ Pull the steaks straight out of the fridge and throw them on the hotplate while it's still heating up.

✘ Grab the tongs, turn that steak and keep turning it. (I can hear you now: 'It's my barbecue, they're my tongs and they're my bloody steaks, so I'll turn them as much as I want to. And if nature calls or fresh beers are required, then I'll hand the tongs over to a mate and make him responsible for turning the poor bloody steaks as many times as possible until I return!' Sorry, but you're just going to have to get over it.)

✘ Throw the steaks back on the same plate that you carried them to the barbecue on, to save on washing up.

✘ Then serve them straightaway and tell everyone to tuck in. You beauty!

Here's a better way:

✔ Firstly, buy the best quality meat you can afford. We're all dead too long to eat rubbish. And use your melon when thinking about the thickness of your steaks. It's hard to get a rare steak with a nice caramelised crust if you start with something just 1 cm thick. If you want a well-done steak and you go the macho 5 cm-thick lump of meat, the outside will be incinerated before the middle is even pink. A 2–3 cm-thick piece is perfect for a medium–rare steak with a lovely crust on the outside.

✔ If you pour oil all over the grillplate, you'll just get lots of burnt oil (if you pour oil all over the chargrill, you're barking mad). Try pouring some oil on a plate, seasoning the steaks with salt and pepper and dipping both sides of each steak into the oil before you cook it.

✔ Take the meat out of the fridge in time for it to return to room temperature before cooking (about 30 minutes will do, covered, and not in the blazing sun). If the meat is cold when it hits the barbie, the outside will cook but the middle will still be raw.

✔ *TURN THE BLOODY STEAKS ONCE.* If you keep turning them, the outsides don't get to seal and caramelise, and you get pale, tough and dry meat.

✔ Make sure your grillplate is hot when the meat goes on or it will stick like glue. If you're cooking a thick-ish steak, you might then want to lower the heat to medium for more even cooking.

✔ When the steaks are done, put them on a clean plate, not the one with the raw meat juices on it.

✔ Rest the meat, loosely covered with foil, for at least 5 minutes to allow all the juices to settle back into the fibres of the meat instead of running all over your plate. Don't seal the foil around the edges of the plate, or the meat will continue to cook in the steam it creates.

✔ Clean your barbie after you cook on it by scraping off the leftover meaty bits and fat with a clean paint scraper or a barbecue spatula. Then remove and wash the grill with warm soapy water and rinse clean. Wash it again before you use it the next time, especially if you don't barbecue very often.

To kick things off

Grilled prawns with Thai dipping sauce

The biggest mistake you can make with seafood on the barbecue is to overcook it. Prawns aren't cheap, so don't ruin them by leaving them on too long. If they're firm to the touch and opaque, they're done. The only other problem you might have with these is making enough to satisfy your friends.

Palm sugar is available in some large supermarkets with special Asian sections, or in any Asian food store.

16 large green (raw) king prawns
2 cloves garlic, crushed
2 tablespoons fish sauce
2 tablespoons neutral oil (see page 10)

THAI DIPPING SAUCE
½ cup lime juice
½ cup fish sauce
2 teaspoons grated palm sugar
1 clove garlic, crushed
2 teaspoons very finely chopped
   coriander leaves
2 bird's-eye chillies,
   de-seeded and very finely chopped

To prepare the prawns, twist off the head and, with a sharp knife, make a 5 mm-deep cut through the back of the shell. Pull out the dark intestinal vein and peel off the shell, leaving on the last section of tail if desired.

In a bowl, combine the prawns with the garlic, fish sauce and oil and marinate, covered with plastic film, in the fridge for an hour. Mix all the dipping sauce ingredients together in another bowl and reserve.

Drain any excess marinade from the prawns and place them on a preheated flat grillplate or chargrill, turning after just a minute. Once they are opaque and firm to the touch, get them off straight away.

Serve the prawns immediately with the dipping sauce – and remind your guests there's no double dipping!

Serves 8

Shellfish in white wine and garlic

You can serve this with pasta as a main course for four people, but it's simpler sans pasta, just with crusty bread and lots of crisp young riesling or semillon. It is such a wonderfully easy and delicious dish. You can mix up the shellfish as below, or just use a couple of kilos of mussels. Try to find Kinkawooka Boston Bay mussels and clams for this dish – they're a farmed, vacuum-packed variety available in supermarkets, with lots of lovely sweet meat in them (steer clear of green-lipped mussels, those big chewy Kiwi things).

2 tablespoons olive oil
3 cloves garlic, finely sliced
750 g small black mussels, 'beards'
   removed, any open shells discarded
750 g clams
750 g pipis
½ cup white wine
½ cup chopped flat-leaf parsley
freshly ground black pepper, to taste

Heat the oil in a large stockpot with a lid or in the baking dish of your barbie. (If your baking dish does not have a lid, you can close the hood of the barbecue instead.)

Add the garlic, and when this starts to sizzle, throw in all the shellfish and the wine. Cover and leave to cook for 2 minutes, then add the parsley and some black pepper, giving the shellfish a gentle stir. Cover and cook for a minute or so more. If most of the shells have opened, the shellfish are cooked – don't overcook the lot by waiting for a few rogue shells to open.

Transfer to six small bowls and serve straight away with crusty bread.

If you want to serve this as a main course with pasta, just mix enough cooked and well-drained spaghetti for four people through the shellfish. Serve with crusty bread and a green salad.

Serves 6

Figs with prosciutto and bocconcini

It seems so long ago now that the ingredients in this dish were considered exotic, let alone difficult to find. These days you can get them just about anywhere.

Whatever you do, don't use mozzarella pizza cheese in place of bocconcini – it tastes like plastic.

8 small fresh bocconcini (sometimes
   called milk cherries), cut in half
16 small basil leaves
4 medium or 8 small fresh figs,
   cut into quarters (or halves if small)
freshly ground black pepper, to taste
4 paper-thin slices prosciutto, sliced into
   four even pieces, each about 5 cm long

Place a piece of cheese and a basil leaf on top of each piece of fig, grind a little black pepper over them, wrap in a slice of prosciutto and secure with a toothpick if necessary. Arrange on a platter and watch them disappear.

Serves 8 (16 bite-sized pieces)

Figs with prosciutto
and bocconcini

Oysters with
gazpacho dressing

Oysters with gazpacho dressing

The purists will tell you the only way to eat oysters is natural, as these salty morsels seem to get as many unsuitable toppings as a pizza these days (tandoori chicken pizza, anyone?).

A nice flavoursome dressing can bring out the best in an oyster, but the thing you should always be a purist about is getting fresh oysters. If you can buy them unopened and shuck them yourself (don't dare rinse them!), you'll really taste the difference.

12 fresh oysters, shucked

GAZPACHO DRESSING
1 teaspoon each very finely diced red onion,
 red capsicum, cucumber (peeled and de-seeded)
 and tomato (peeled and de-seeded)
1 tablespoon olive oil
1 tablespoon sherry vinegar
a few drops Tabasco sauce
freshly ground black pepper, to taste

Place all the dressing ingredients in a screw-top container and shake, then chill the dressing in the fridge for 30 minutes. Spoon a little of the dressing onto each oyster and serve.

Serves 4

Guacamole

More often than not, guacamole is a sanitised, bland bowl of green mush. Spice it up! A good guacamole should have enough oomph to make you want to drink more beer – rarely a bad thing.

We can't get fresh Mexican chillies in Australia, but it's better to get the flavour of fresh chillies than use dried imports. This recipe uses 2 large chillies but you can adjust the amount according to your own chilli threshold. Try jalapenos if you can find them, as they add a lovely fruity flavour.

2 large ripe avocados, peeled and stones removed
1 medium red onion, very finely chopped
2 large red or green chillies, de-seeded and finely chopped
1 large ripe tomato, de-seeded and finely chopped
2 tablespoons finely chopped coriander leaves
2 tablespoons olive oil
juice of 1 lime
generous dash Tabasco sauce
sea salt and freshly ground black pepper, to taste

Chop or lightly mash the avocados (depending on how chunky you like your dip) and transfer to a serving bowl. Mix in the rest of the ingredients and serve with plain corn chips and plenty of cold beer.

Serves 6–8

Mini toasted cheese
sambos – three ways

You can pre-assemble these little beauties beforehand and throw them on a very clean, preheated flat grillplate when your guests arrive. Make sure the grill isn't too hot, because you want the cheese to melt before the outsides get too brown.

butter, for spreading
1 good-quality baguette, cut into slices
   a little less than 1 cm thick
3 bocconcini, sliced
4 pieces semi-dried tomatoes,
   finely chopped (about 2 tablespoons)
2 thin slices leg ham, cut to fit on the
   baguette slices
4 tablespoons grated gruyère cheese
8 slices haloumi cheese, halved crossways
2 tablespoons finely chopped mint

Butter the baguette slices, and fill about one-third of them (buttered-side out) with bocconcini and tomato, one-third with ham and gruyère, and the last third with haloumi and mint. (You'll get an idea of quantities and whether you need more bread when you have your first crack at these.)

Cook the sambos over low heat on a preheated flat grillplate until the outsides are golden brown and the cheese inside is soft and gooey. Flatten slightly with the back of a spatula when you turn them. Yum!

Serves 8 (watch out though, these are quite filling)

Crudités with dipping sauces

Raw vegetables mightn't be very blokey, but it's good to have something light to start with on a stinking hot day. These three sauces have such contrasting flavours: the lemon mayo is creamy and citrussy; the edamame dip is light and sweet; and the tapenade is big, bold and salty.

Packets of frozen edamame (green soy beans) can be found in most Asian food stores.

LEMON MAYO

1 egg yolk

½ teaspoon Dijon mustard

1 cup olive oil

1 teaspoon lemon juice

1 teaspoon finely grated lemon zest

EDAMAME DIP

200 g frozen edamame (green soy beans)
   cooked as per instructions on packet,
   then shelled and pods discarded

1 small clove garlic, sliced

4 mint leaves, torn

1 tablespoon lime juice

½ teaspoon sugar

sea salt and freshly ground black pepper, to taste

¼ cup olive oil

TAPENADE

1 cup pitted black olives

1 large clove garlic, sliced

4 anchovy fillets in oil, drained

10 basil leaves, torn

2–3 tablespoons olive oil

an assortment of very fresh, preferably baby,
   vegetables such as carrots, zucchini, radishes,
   asparagus, celery, cucumber and beetroot

For the lemon mayo, use an electric mixer to beat the egg yolk and mustard together, adding the oil drop by drop at first until the mayo thickens, and then in a thin stream until you have a thick, eggy consistency. Add the lemon juice and zest, then mix for just a second more.

To make the edamame dip, combine all the ingredients except the oil in a food processor, then gradually add enough oil to produce a thick paste that's not too firm.

And lastly, for the tapenade, use a food processor or hand-held blender to combine the olives, garlic, anchovies and basil until you have a very thick paste. Gradually add just enough oil to give the consistency of a dip.

To prepare the crudités, peel the vegetables, if necessary, then cut into bite-sized pieces.

Serve the crudités very cold (preferably on ice) on a large platter, surrounded by the dipping sauces.

Makes enough to feed a small army

Prawns wrapped in prosciutto with a jalapeno butter sauce

Wrapping chicken, beef, seafood or vegetables such as asparagus in prosciutto is a great way to add salty character to any dish. The fat in the prosciutto also means that you won't need to use any oil on the barbecue plate.

12 large green (raw) king prawns
12 thin slices prosciutto

JALAPENO BUTTER SAUCE
6 cloves garlic
1 large onion, finely chopped
4–6 red jalapeno chillies *or* 3 medium
  red chillies, de-seeded and chopped
2 tablespoons olive oil
1 kg very ripe tomatoes, chopped
1 tablespoon brown sugar
1 tablespoon balsamic vinegar
150 g cold butter, chopped

To make the sauce, first place the garlic cloves (in their skins) in a small roasting dish, and roast in a 200°C oven for about 10 minutes, or until soft. Peel the skins off while the garlic is still warm.

In a heavy-based saucepan, fry the onion and chillies in the oil over moderate heat. When the onion is translucent, add the tomato, roasted garlic and brown sugar. Cook for about 30 minutes, until the tomato is completely broken up. Remove the pan from the heat and purée the mixture with a hand-held blender, then push the sauce through a coarse sieve. Return the sauce to the pan and reheat to a gentle simmer, then remove from the heat and stir in the balsamic vinegar and butter.

To prepare the prawns, twist off the head and, with a sharp knife, make a 5 mm-deep cut through the back of the shell. Pull out the dark intestinal vein and peel off the shell, leaving on the last section of tail if desired.

Wrap each prawn in a slice of prosciutto, and cook on a preheated flat grillplate or chargrill until the prosciutto is crisp and the prawns are opaque and firm to the touch.

Divide the sauce between four plates and pile the prawns on top. Serve with grilled corn cobs cut into rounds.

Serves 4

Vegetable frittata

If you can make one type of frittata, you can make a hundred. Red capsicum and cooked fresh corn, leek and coriander or caramelised onion and rosemary can easily be substituted for the vegetables and parsley used here.

For an alternative to pan-frying, spoon the mixture into a non-stick silicone baking tray and bake in a 200°C oven for about 15 minutes, or until just set. Turn out immediately.

Cut the frittata into small pieces to serve 12 as finger food.

1 onion, very finely sliced
1 carrot, grated
1 zucchini, grated
1 teaspoon neutral oil (see page 10)
8 free-range or organic eggs
½ cup flat-leaf parsley, chopped
½ cup grated parmesan or gruyère cheese
1 teaspoon butter

Fry the onion, carrot and zucchini in the oil in a non-stick 12–14 cm frying pan until soft. Transfer to a bowl and allow to cool slightly. Wipe the pan clean.

Break the eggs into a bowl and beat with a fork, add the parsley and cheese, then fold through the cooked vegetables. Melt the butter in the pan over a very low heat, then pour in the egg mixture. Put the lid on or cover tightly with foil and cook for 10 minutes, then uncover and continue to cook for another 10 minutes. The trick is to cook the frittata through without burning the bottom.

Slide the frittata out of the pan and slice. Serve at room temperature or cold.

Serves 6

Chargrilled octopus salad

The 1980s may not have had a lot going for them, but they were when Australian restaurants decided that grilled baby octopus was the epitome of flash. They went out of fashion as quickly as they came in, and now only baggy-arse places seem to serve them, which is crazy, because if you can get locally caught octopus with their tentacles curled under them (an indicator of freshness), they're delicious.

The ideal octopus for the barbie has a body of about 4 cm diameter or a total width of about 8–10 cm.

12 baby octopus, heads and hard beaks removed, left whole or cut in half
3 cloves garlic, crushed or very finely sliced
2 tablespoons olive oil
1 red onion, very finely sliced
16–20 ripe cherry or grape tomatoes, cut in half
1 bunch rocket (baby or wild), washed and dried
1 medium cucumber, peeled, then sliced or cubed

SALAD DRESSING
½ cup olive oil
¼ cup balsamic vinegar
sea salt and freshly ground black pepper, to taste
1 red chilli, de-seeded and finely chopped (optional)

Place the octopus, garlic and 2 tablespoons of oil in a ceramic or stainless steel bowl. Mix well, cover with plastic film and marinate for 2–12 hours in the fridge. Bring the octopus to room temperature by removing from the fridge 15 minutes before cooking.

Just prior to cooking the octopus, mix the dressing ingredients in the base of a large bowl and toss with the onion, tomatoes, rocket and cucumber.

Preheat your flat grillplate or chargrill to very hot, then cook the octopus for a couple of minutes either side, until just opaque and firm to the touch.

Toss the cooked octopus through the salad and serve.

Serves 4 generously

Chargrilled octopus salad

Mussels in tomato and chilli sauce

The amount of chillies that you use here is entirely up to you. If you want to really spice things up, use the small but very hot bird's-eye variety.

2 cloves garlic, roughly chopped
1 small onion, sliced
3 tablespoons olive oil
4 very ripe tomatoes, chopped
2–3 medium chillies, de-seeded and finely sliced
2 kg black mussels, 'beards' removed, any open
    shells discarded
12 basil leaves, very finely sliced
12 flat-leaf parsley leaves, finely sliced
freshly ground black pepper, to taste

In a large stockpot with a lid, soften the garlic and onion in the oil over high heat. Add the tomatoes and chillies and cook over medium heat for about 10 minutes, until the tomatoes have broken down. Remove the pot from the heat, and purée the mixture with a hand-held blender.

Return the pot to the flame and turn the heat to high. Add the mussels, placing the lid on the pot immediately. Cook for 3 minutes, shaking the pot occasionally. Check that the mussels have opened – cook for a minute or two more if most have not. The total cooking time should be between 3–5 minutes. Add the fresh herbs and black pepper, and serve immediately with crusty bread.

Serves 6

Clams with prosciutto, chilli, mint and sherry

There isn't much meat on a clam, so this dish is more about flavours than a full tummy, and it's a terrific prelude to a nice big steak.

The clams used here are a farmed variety available vacuum-packed in supermarkets (see page 16).

1 large clove garlic, finely diced
½ large red chilli, de-seeded and finely diced
½ red capsicum, white insides and
    seeds removed, finely diced
2 red shallots, peeled and finely diced
4 thin slices prosciutto, finely diced
2 tablespoons olive oil
2 kg Kinkawooka Boston Bay clams
    or live clams if available
¼ cup dry sherry
16 mint leaves, finely shredded
freshly ground black pepper, to taste

In a stockpot or large heavy-based saucepan with a tight-fitting lid, fry the garlic, chilli, capsicum, shallots and prosciutto in the oil over high heat for a minute or two, without browning the vegetables.

Add the clams and sherry, then immediately place the lid on the pot. Check after a few minutes to see if all the shells are opened – if not, give them a minute more. If most of the shells have opened, the clams are cooked – don't overcook the lot by waiting for a few rogue shells to open.

Stir through the mint and some black pepper, then pile into four bowls, spooning over all the juices.

Serve with some thinly sliced baguette to sop up the sweet and salty juices – they're far too good to waste.

Serves 4

Clams with prosciutto,
chilli, mint and sherry

Grilled corn
with lime butter

Corn is a vegetable that works gangbusters on the barbecue. You can strip the cobs of their husks and silks and cook them as they are, just topping them with a knob of butter when they are done. Or you can dust them first with some Great Aussie Barbie Spice Rub (see page 110), or a ready-made Moroccan or Cajun spice mix, to form a nice spicy crust.

This recipe introduces the butter at the start of the cooking process, so the flavour permeates right through the corn. It is more of an entrée than an accompaniment.

6 corn cobs, silks removed but
husks left on

LIME BUTTER
150 g butter, softened
1 clove garlic, crushed
zest of two limes, very finely grated
1 teaspoon freshly ground black pepper
2 teaspoons lime juice
2 teaspoons very finely chopped chives

Mix all the lime butter ingredients together in a bowl. Carefully open the corn husks and spread the butter over the cobs with a knife, then reseal them as best you can and twist the ends to secure.

Place the cobs on a preheated chargrill for about 20 minutes, turning every few minutes, until the kernels are tender. Serve piping hot and eat with the butter dripping down your arms.

Serves a very messy but happy 6

Barbecued octopus with hummus

Here's another easy dish using baby octopus. You prepare and cook the octopus the same way as for the Chargrilled Octopus Salad (see page 26), but match it instead with a splendidly garlicky hummus.

Tahini is widely available in large supermarkets and specialty delis.

8 baby octopus, heads and hard beaks
    removed, left whole or cut in half
2 cloves garlic, crushed
2 tablespoons olive oil
2 tablespoons fresh oregano or marjoram leaves
1 lemon, cut into wedges, to garnish

HUMMUS
200 g chickpeas, soaked in cold water
    overnight, then boiled until tender
    (about 2 hours) and drained *or* 2 × 400 g
    cans chickpeas, drained and rinsed
2 cloves garlic, crushed
¼ cup extra virgin olive oil
1 tablespoon tahini (sesame paste)
1 tablespoon lemon juice
sea salt, to taste

Place the octopus, garlic and olive oil in a bowl and marinate, covered with plastic film, in the fridge for 2–12 hours. Bring the octopus to room temperature by removing from the fridge 15 minutes before cooking.

To make the hummus, place all the ingredients in a food processor and blend until smooth. Gradually add enough water to form a thick purée.

Preheat your flat grillplate or chargrill to very hot, then cook the octopus for a couple of minutes on each side, until just opaque and firm to the touch.

To serve, spoon a dollop of hummus onto each of four plates and place two octopus on top. Sprinkle with the oregano or marjoram leaves and garnish with lemon wedges, drizzling a little extra virgin olive oil over the top if you like.

Serves 4

Scallops with sauce vierge

You could find this dish in some of the very best restaurants in Paris, but it adapts perfectly to the Aussie barbecue. Look for the large roe-less Queensland scallops when they come into season in late October.

16–20 fresh scallops, hard sinew
    removed, shells cleaned and reserved
½ teaspoon olive oil
sea salt and freshly ground black
    pepper, to taste
16 leaves/sprigs of chives, chervil
    and tarragon, to garnish

SAUCE VIERGE
⅓ cup extra virgin olive oil
1 tablespoon lemon juice
1 teaspoon coriander seeds, crushed
8 basil leaves, finely sliced
2 medium ripe tomatoes, peeled,
    de-seeded and diced

To make the sauce, gently warm the oil in a saucepan, but do not boil. Remove from the heat and mix in the lemon juice, coriander, basil and tomato. Set aside while you cook the scallops.

Coat the scallops in the oil and season lightly with salt and pepper. Preheat your flat grillplate to very hot, then sear the scallops until just cooked – no more than a minute each side. They should be opaque in the middle.

Arrange the clean scallop shells on a large serving platter, and drizzle some sauce in each. Place a scallop on top, garnish with the fresh herbs, and serve immediately.

Serves 4

Scallops with sauce vierge

Spicy minute beef
in lettuce cups

The only 'spicy' here is from the ginger, and the kids will love putting a spoonful of this and that in their lettuce leaf before demolishing it. You can cheat a bit by buying ready-cut stir-fry strips of beef.

Throw everything in the middle of the table and invite your guests to help themselves.

500 g rump or sirloin steak
4 cloves garlic, crushed
1 knob ginger (about 3 cm long), grated
¼ cup light soy sauce
2 teaspoons sesame oil
1 tablespoon sugar
½ cup sesame seeds
200 g rice vermicelli noodles
2 tablespoons neutral oil (see page 10)
1 butter lettuce, leaves removed and
  washed, dried and chilled
1 cup finely sliced spring onions
  (dark green part only)

Slice the meat as thinly as possible, removing all the fat. Mix the garlic, ginger, soy sauce, 1 teaspoon of the sesame oil and the sugar together in a bowl, and marinate the meat in this mixture, covered with plastic film, in the fridge for 2–12 hours.

Toast the sesame seeds by placing them in a hot frying pan with no oil or butter for a minute or two, shaking the pan from time to time, until they are golden brown. (Be careful – they can go from golden brown to burnt in the time it takes to sip a beer.)

Place the noodles in a bowl of very hot water for 5 minutes, then drain well and mix with the remaining teaspoon of sesame oil.

Preheat the flat grillplate of your barbecue to very hot. Drizzle the neutral oil over the grillplate to cover it. Spread the meat out over the oiled plate and cook for around 30 seconds each side.

Place the meat in a bowl in the middle of the table along with separate bowls of the noodles, lettuce leaves, spring onions and toasted sesame seeds. Invite your guests to take a lettuce leaf and fill with some noodles, beef, a few spring onions and a sprinkling of sesame seeds, drizzling the lot with sweet chilli sauce, if desired, before rolling up and eating.

Serves 6

Things on
bread and sticks

Easy turmeric chicken skewers

Some things on sticks are a lot of work. Happily though, these Indian-spiced skewers take no time at all to make, and the flavours are mild enough for even the tin lids to enjoy.

5 boneless chicken thighs
   (about 120 g each), trimmed of
   excess fat and cut into 2.5 cm pieces
8 bamboo skewers
lime wedges, to garnish

MARINADE
2 teaspoons dried turmeric
½ teaspoon ground cumin
½ teaspoon ground coriander
1 teaspoon salt
1 tablespoon lime juice
1 tablespoon neutral oil (see page 10)

Combine the marinade ingredients together with the chicken pieces in a shallow dish, cover with plastic film, and marinate in the fridge for 4–12 hours.

Soak the bamboo skewers in water for 1 hour before use to prevent them from burning. Bring the chicken to room temperature by removing from the fridge half an hour before cooking.

Thread the chicken pieces onto the bamboo skewers, and cook on a preheated flat grillplate or chargrill until the chicken is cooked through.

Garnish with lime wedges and serve.

Serves 4

Rosemary lamb skewers

If you are lucky enough to have a rosemary bush growing in your backyard or nearby, using the stalks as skewers for your meat is a great little party trick. If you can't get enough rosemary for this, don't pay an exorbitant amount for art-directed stalks from a 'boutique' kitchen shop: just use bamboo or metal skewers instead.

Bamboo skewers need to be soaked in water for 1 hour before use to prevent them from burning.

1 kg boneless lamb leg or shoulder, trimmed
   of excess fat and cut into 2 cm cubes
½ cup good-quality olive oil
3 cloves garlic, crushed
1 teaspoon finely grated lemon zest
1 tablespoon finely chopped rosemary leaves
8–12 thick rosemary stalks (about 14 cm long)
1 tablespoon sea salt
1 teaspoon freshly ground black pepper
lemon wedges, to garnish

Combine the lamb, oil, garlic, lemon zest and chopped rosemary in a shallow bowl, cover with plastic film, and marinate in the fridge for 2–12 hours. Bring the meat to room temperature by removing from the fridge half an hour before cooking.

If using rosemary stalks as skewers, cut a diagonal slice off the woody end so you have a sharp point to push through the meat.

Season the marinated meat with salt and pepper and stir through, then thread two or three pieces of lamb onto each rosemary skewer. If you have trouble threading the meat on, carefully pierce through each piece with a metal skewer and then slide onto the rosemary stalk. Cook on a preheated flat grillplate or chargrill over medium heat for a few minutes each side, until done to your liking. Garnish with lemon wedges and serve immediately.

Serves 4–6

Rosemary
lamb skewers

The Great Aussie Hamburger

Some things are sacred. The Great Aussie Hamburger is one of them.

The genuine article always contains a beef pattie, fried onions, a slice of tomato, shredded iceberg lettuce, too much barbecue or tomato sauce, iodised salt (but no pepper), and of course, canned beetroot. All served on a daggy white toasted bun, ideally in a milk bar.

Acceptable variations include bacon and fried egg (for one with 'the lot'), a slice of plastic cheese (for a cheeseburger), and canned pineapple (for nostalgic reasons, but only if you must).

neutral oil (see page 10), for grilling
400 g minced beef
1 large brown onion, very thinly sliced
4 hamburger buns
butter, for spreading
1–2 cups finely shredded iceberg lettuce
4 large slices tomato
4 large slices canned beetroot
salt, to taste
barbecue or tomato sauce, to taste

Preheat a flat grillplate and pour on a little oil. Divide the meat into four balls, place on the hot grillplate, and flatten them with a barbecue spatula. Make the patties as big as possible because they will shrink a little as they cook.

At the same time, add a little more oil and fry the onions until soft. Either toast the buns or grill them over a medium flame on the chargrill.

Butter the bottom half of the bun and arrange the 'salad' on it: first the lettuce, then the tomato and beetroot slices.

Once cooked, place the beef and onions on top of the salad, add a liberal dose of salt and plenty of sauce, then top with the bun lid. (There is no such thing as an 'open' hamburger – it's café/bistro bollocks.)

Serve with some greasy chips if possible.

Serves 4 magnificently

Thai prawn skewers

In the spirit of the times, this recipe recycles the marinade used to flavour the prawns and transforms it into a delicious sauce. A really important note: never serve a marinade in this way unless it has been boiled to eliminate any bacteria from the raw shellfish or meat, otherwise you run the risk of poisoning your guests and most likely ruining their day.

24 medium green (raw) king prawns
12 bamboo skewers
2 tablespoons finely chopped coriander
leaves, to garnish
lime wedges, to garnish

MARINADE
4 coriander roots and first 1 cm
of stems, well rinsed
1 stalk lemongrass (bottom section only,
outer layers removed), finely sliced
1 bird's-eye or medium red chilli,
de-seeded and chopped
2 cloves garlic, chopped
1 teaspoon finely grated ginger
2 teaspoons grated palm sugar
⅓ cup lime juice
¼ cup fish sauce
300 ml coconut milk

To make the marinade, blend the coriander roots, lemongrass, chilli, garlic, ginger and palm sugar in a food processor until smooth, then add the lime juice, fish sauce and coconut milk and blend a little more to combine.

To prepare the prawns, twist off the head and, with a sharp knife, make a 5 mm-deep cut through the back of the shell. Pull out the dark intestinal vein and peel off the shell, leaving on the last section of tail if desired.

Place the prawns in a shallow bowl and pour the marinade over, making sure the prawns are well coated. Cover with plastic film and refrigerate for 2–4 hours. Soak the bamboo skewers in water for 1 hour before use to prevent them from burning.

Bring the prawns to room temperature by removing from the fridge 15 minutes before cooking. Preheat your chargrill to hot, then thread two prawns onto each skewer and cook for just a minute or so on either side, until firm to the touch and opaque. Meanwhile, drain the marinade into a saucepan and bring to the boil, then simmer over high heat for 1 minute.

Serve the skewers on a platter and pour over the hot marinade. Garnish with chopped coriander and lime wedges, and serve.

Serves 4 as a snack or starter

Leftover roast beef rolls

These are a smart way to use up the meat leftover from last night's roast – they're disgustingly rich and so yummy that you'll soon find yourself making twice as much roast beef as you need to make sure you have plenty left for this dish.

1 large onion, very thinly sliced
2 tablespoons neutral oil (see page 10)
8–12 leftover roast beef slices, cut as thin as
    possible, *or* some shaved roast beef from your deli
½ cup ready-made beef or veal stock, diluted
    with ½ cup water
2 tablespoons finely chopped flat-leaf parsley
4 crispy Italian-style bread rolls, buttered
sea salt and freshly ground black pepper, to taste

Preheat your flat grillplate to medium and cook the onion in the oil. Once the onion is soft, add the thinly sliced beef and toss for a few seconds to warm through.

Slowly pour the stock over the onion and beef, and add the parsley. Cook, stirring together, for a minute or so to allow the stock to reduce slightly and the beef to absorb the flavours.

Divide the mixture between the four bread rolls. Season with salt and pepper and serve.

Serves 4

The Great Aussie Steak Sambo

There are plenty of delicious recipes for meat on bread, but just like the Great Aussie Hamburger, there's only one Great Aussie Steak Sambo.

This is the simplified footy-club version, which omits all of the green healthy stuff and just sticks to the basics (altered slightly to spare you the home-brand margarine and stewing meat they use at the football).

1 large brown onion, thinly sliced
neutral oil (see page 10), for grilling
4 thin slices beef scotch fillet
8 slices thick white bread, buttered
lots of tomato or barbecue sauce
salt, to taste

Cook the onions in the oil on a preheated flat grillplate. If they start to dry out and burn, add a little liquid – beer is often close by at a barbecue.

After about 3 minutes, when the onions are almost cooked, throw the steaks on a screaming hot chargrill, and cook them until nicely brown on the outside and slightly pink in the centre, turning them once.

Serve the steak and onions between two slices of bread, adding sauce and salt to taste.

In keeping with footy-club tradition, serve the sambos on pieces of cheap kitchen paper instead of plates, so they drip all over everyone's laps.

Serves 4

The Great Aussie
Steak Sambo

Steak and barbecue sauce rolls – the hard way

There's not a lot wrong with your traditional steak sambo with onions and ready-made barbecue sauce. However, this variation is definitely worth the extra effort: the steak gets a quick spice rub beforehand and then has a dip in homemade barbecue sauce, making it even more delicious. But be warned, the flavours are highly addictive.

4 thin slices sirloin beef or scotch fillet
⅓ cup neutral oil (see page 10)
1 large onion, thinly sliced
4 soft hamburger, damper or hot dog rolls,
    large enough to fit the steak in

SPICE RUB
2 teaspoons paprika
2 teaspoons celery salt
¼ teaspoon cayenne pepper

BARBECUE SAUCE
1 cup tomato sauce
1 tablespoon brown sugar
¼ teaspoon cayenne pepper
2 tablespoons Worcestershire sauce
2 tablespoons cider vinegar
½ teaspoon mustard powder

Combine all the sauce ingredients together in your wok and bring to the boil, then simmer on low heat for a couple of minutes.

Mix the spice rub ingredients together and sprinkle over both sides of the steaks. Cook the steaks in half the oil on a preheated flat grillplate for a couple of minutes either side. When you turn the steaks, add the remaining oil to the grillplate and cook the onions in it for 2–3 minutes until soft, adding a little water or beer if they start to burn.

When cooked, transfer the steaks and onions to the wok and simmer in the sauce for a minute or two.

Serve a piece of steak and plenty of onions in each roll, and spoon the barbecue sauce over the top.

Serves 4

Yakitori

It seems a million years ago now, but there was a time when yakitori was the exotic fare of the serious Japanese restaurant. Now it's everywhere – on sushi trains, in food halls and hole-in-the-wall suburban Japanese takeaways. None of which makes it any less yummy.

You'll find sake and mirin in Asian supermarkets.

2 chicken breasts (about 300 g each)
    or 4 boneless chicken thighs (about 140 g each),
    trimmed of excess fat and cut into 2 cm cubes
12 bamboo skewers
4 spring onions (white and pale green parts only),
    trimmed and cut into 2 cm lengths

MARINADE
1 tablespoon sugar
¼ cup sake
¼ cup soy sauce
2 tablespoons mirin

Mix the marinade ingredients with the chicken in a shallow bowl, cover with plastic film, and marinate in the fridge for 2 hours. Soak the bamboo skewers in water for 1 hour before use to prevent them from burning.

Bring the chicken to room temperature by removing from the fridge half an hour before cooking.

Thread the chicken and spring onion pieces onto the skewers, reserving the marinade.

Cook the skewers on a preheated chargrill over medium heat, brushing now and then with the reserved marinade, until the chicken is cooked through. To serve the marinade as a sauce, bring it to the boil in a small saucepan, simmer for at least a minute, and pour it over the skewers before serving.

Serves 4 as a snack or starter

Yakitori

Lemongrass chicken sticks

If you can't be bothered to dig out the food processor, consider using the real thing – a mortar and pestle. A quick trip to Chinatown or a specialty food market should get you one for around $40–60. Make sure you get quite a big one and make sure it's the last thing you buy – you won't want to carry it around for long.

Palm sugar is available in some large supermarkets with special Asian sections, or in any Asian food store.

3 stalks lemongrass (bottom section only, outer layers removed), finely sliced
2 cloves garlic, sliced
1 medium red chilli, de-seeded and sliced
2 red shallots or spring onions (white part only), finely sliced
few drops neutral oil (see page 10)
1 tablespoon honey
1 tablespoon fish sauce
1 tablespoon oyster sauce
1 teaspoon sesame oil
1 teaspoon grated palm sugar
5 boneless chicken thighs (about 600 g), trimmed of excess fat and cut into 2 cm pieces
8 bamboo skewers

Make a paste from the lemongrass, garlic, chilli and red shallots or spring onions using a mortar and pestle or food processor, adding a few drops of oil if necessary.

Transfer the paste to a shallow bowl and add the honey, fish sauce, oyster sauce, sesame oil and sugar, and mix well. Fold the chicken pieces through, making sure they are completely coated with the marinade, then cover with plastic film and marinate in the fridge for 2–4 hours.

Soak the bamboo skewers in water for 1 hour before use to prevent them from burning.

Bring the chicken to room temperature by removing from the fridge half an hour before cooking. Preheat your flat grillplate or chargrill to hot, then thread the chicken pieces onto bamboo skewers and cook for a few minutes each side, or until the chicken is completely cooked through. Arrange on a platter and let your guests tuck in.

Serves 4 as a snack or starter

Spicy pork tortillas with salsa

This dish goes really well with a Saturday-arvo footy match on the TV. You will need to prepare the pork the night before or the morning of the match and put it on to cook about 4½ hours before kick-off. Turn the barbie off as the game starts and the meat will be perfect by half-time.

2–3 kg boned pork shoulder,
  trimmed of skin and excess fat
8–12 tortillas

SPICE RUB
1 teaspoon paprika
1 teaspoon mustard powder
1 teaspoon dried thyme
2 teaspoons brown sugar
½ teaspoon cayenne pepper,
  or a little more to taste
2 teaspoons celery salt
1 teaspoon freshly ground black pepper
1 teaspoon onion powder

SALSA
½ cup diced tomato flesh,
  seeds and juice removed
½ cup finely chopped red onion
½ cup diced green capsicum
½ cup diced peach, mango or nectarine
1–2 chillies, de-seeded and very finely diced
2 tablespoons lime juice
2 tablespoons olive oil
⅔ cup chopped coriander leaves
freshly ground black pepper, to taste

Place the pork in a shallow dish, mix all the spice rub ingredients together, and rub into the pork. Cover with plastic film and marinate in the fridge for 4–24 hours.

Bring the pork to room temperature by removing from the fridge half an hour before cooking. Transfer to a baking dish, and place the dish on a rack in the middle of your preheated barbecue, making sure the heat is surrounding the meat on both sides but is not directly underneath, then close the hood and cook for 2 hours. Open the hood and cook for another 2 hours, basting every 30 minutes with the meat juices from the pan.

Remove the dish from the barbecue and set aside to rest, loosely covered in foil, for 20–30 minutes before serving.

To prepare the salsa, mix all the ingredients together in a serving bowl and store in the fridge.

If you would like to serve the tortillas warm, throw them on the flat grillplate for a few seconds each side just before serving. Use two forks to lightly shred the pork, and serve topped with plenty of salsa in the warmed tortillas.

Serves 6

Lamb koftas
with spicy yoghurt

Koftas are a classic barbecue dish, and there's no shortage of variations. This one combines minced lamb and onion with herbs and garlic, and there's a spicy yoghurt to go with it for some extra zing.

You can use either bamboo or metal skewers for this – if using bamboo ones, soak them in water for 1 hour before use to prevent them from burning.

12 bamboo or metal skewers

KOFTAS
1 kg lamb mince
1 clove garlic, crushed
1 medium onion, very finely chopped
1 teaspoon salt
½ teaspoon freshly ground black pepper
2 tablespoons finely chopped fresh coriander leaves
2 tablespoons finely chopped fresh mint leaves
1 tablespoon ground paprika
1 tablespoon ground cumin
1 tablespoon ground coriander
½ teaspoon ground cayenne pepper

SPICY YOGHURT
100 g Greek-style yoghurt
1 clove garlic, crushed
½ teaspoon ground cumin
½ teaspoon each finely chopped coriander, chives and mint
¼ teaspoon ground cayenne pepper
1 teaspoon finely grated lemon zest
1 teaspoon lemon juice
½ teaspoon sea salt
½ teaspoon freshly ground black pepper

Combine all the kofta ingredients in a large bowl, cover with plastic film, and marinate in the fridge for at least 1 hour to allow the flavours to develop.

Mix together all the spicy yoghurt ingredients in a bowl, cover with plastic film, and refrigerate until ready to use.

Divide the lamb mixture into 24 even portions and shape 2 each around a skewer. Place the skewers on a preheated flat grillplate or chargrill and cook for about 10 minutes, turning often (make sure the barbecue is not too hot or they may burn).

To serve, pile the skewers onto a large serving plate with the spicy yoghurt alongside.

Serves 4

Beef-lover's hot
dog with spicy
beef sauce

Beef-lover's hot dog with spicy beef sauce

Some people just can't get enough red meat. So here's an upmarket hot doggie made with a good-quality beef sausage and smothered in spicy meat sauce. Not recommended for vegetarians!

6 good-quality beef sausages

6 long white rolls

SPICY BEEF SAUCE

2 tablespoons olive oil

1 small brown onion, finely chopped

750 g lean minced beef

2 teaspoons paprika

1 teaspoon chilli powder, or to taste

1 cup tomato sauce

1 tablespoon tomato paste

about 1 cup water

sea salt and freshly ground black pepper, to taste

To make the sauce, heat the oil in a wok and add the onion, cooking until soft without browning. Add the beef and stir-fry for a minute or two. Stir in the paprika, chilli powder, tomato sauce, tomato paste and a cup of water, and season with salt and pepper. Bring to the boil, then simmer over a low heat for 30 minutes, adding a little more water if necessary.

While the sauce is simmering, cook the sausages over a low–medium heat on a preheated flat grillplate until just cooked through.

Slice the bread rolls open, place a sausage in each, and top with plenty of meat sauce.

This goes well with very cold beer, inelegant chat, and sport of any kind on the TV.

Serves 6

Greek-style lamb burgers

The Great Aussie Hamburger is a sacred thing. This is not an imitation of the icon, but rather a really tasty alternative with Greek flavours, that also just happens to be meat patties on bread.

It's worth using Turkish bread for Greek burgers to wind up both nationalities.

500 g minced lamb

6 pitted Kalamata olives, very finely chopped

2 teaspoons dried mint

2 teaspoons dried oregano

1 teaspoon sea salt

½ teaspoon pepper

1 tablespoon lemon juice

olive oil, for grilling

4 dessertspoons crumbled fetta cheese

1 loaf Turkish bread, cut into four sections, and sections cut in half lengthwise

a handful of rocket leaves

4 slices tomato

12 thin slices cucumber

4 heaped tablespoons plain yoghurt

sea salt and freshly ground black pepper, to taste

Mix the minced lamb, olives, mint, oregano, salt, pepper and lemon juice together in a bowl, then divide into four even balls. Squash the meat as flat as you can between your hands (or onto a floured work surface) to make large patties 12–15 cm in diameter. Sprinkle some olive oil on a preheated flat grillplate and cook the lamb patties for a few minutes either side, being careful not to overcook them. Place a dessertspoon of crumbled fetta on the cooked side of each pattie as soon as it is turned, so the cheese melts slightly as the meat cooks.

When the patties are almost cooked, toast the Turkish bread on the chargrill, then build the burgers by starting with a slice of toasted bread, then some rocket, a lamb pattie topped with cheese, a slice of tomato, three slices of cucumber and a spoonful of yoghurt. Top with more salt and pepper to taste.

You don't need to serve anything else with this – it's a meal in itself.

Serves 4

Turkish shish kebabs

This is the world's most famous kebab. In this version, the marinade will need at least 12 hours to work its wonders.

The vegetables go on separate skewers because they will take less time to cook, while the lamb is cut in large pieces so it remains nice and tender.

1 kg boneless leg of lamb, cut into 3 cm cubes

12 metal or bamboo skewers

2 medium zucchini, cut into 5 mm-thick slices

1 red onion, cut into 2 cm pieces

1 red capsicum, white insides and
    seeds removed, cut into 2 cm pieces

1 green capsicum, white insides and
    seeds removed, cut into 2 cm pieces

8 cherry tomatoes

MARINADE

200 g plain or Greek-style yoghurt

2 tablespoons olive oil

3 cloves garlic, crushed

1 teaspoon dried chilli flakes

2 teaspoons salt

1 teaspoon freshly ground black pepper

Combine all the marinade ingredients together with the lamb in a shallow bowl, cover with plastic film, and marinate in the fridge for 2–24 hours.

If using bamboo skewers, soak them in water for 1 hour before use to prevent them from burning. Bring the lamb to room temperature by removing from the fridge half an hour before cooking.

Divide the lamb pieces between eight skewers and cook on a preheated chargrill over high heat for about 10 minutes, turning to ensure each side is cooked evenly. While the meat is cooking, divide the vegetables among four skewers, and then cook alongside the meat (the vegetables should be done in around 5 minutes).

Serve two lamb kebabs and one vegetable kebab per person, with pita or Turkish bread.

Serves 4

Feed the man meat

Jamaican steaks

Here's an easy way to spice up a steak. All you need are a few fresh ingredients and some dried spices for flavour and you're away.

The type of chillies that you use will determine the level of heat. Remember, bigger is not necessarily better here, boys – in this case, small is lethal.

4 sirloin steaks, each about 2 cm thick

MARINADE
4 mild medium red chillies *or*
    up to 6 bird's-eye chillies
    if you are so inclined,
    de-seeded and chopped
2 red shallots, peeled and chopped
1 bunch fresh coriander,
    leaves picked and roots washed
½ cup flat-leaf parsley leaves,
    freshly chopped
1 tablespoon ground allspice
1 teaspoon ground cloves
1 teaspoon ground cumin
1 teaspoon ground coriander
1 teaspoon sea salt
1 teaspoon freshly ground black pepper
¼ cup olive oil
2 tablespoons lemon juice

Combine all the marinade ingredients in a food processor or blender, and blend to a smooth paste. Spread the paste over the steaks, then cover the meat and refrigerate for 2–12 hours.

Bring the meat to room temperature by removing from the fridge half an hour before cooking. Preheat your flat grillplate.

Scrape any excess marinade from the steaks, retaining it for basting during cooking.

Place the steaks on the hot grillplate and cook until done to your liking. Brush the reserved marinade over the steaks once or twice whilst cooking.

Remove the steaks and set them aside to rest, loosely covered in foil, for several minutes before serving.

Serves 4

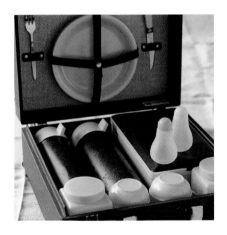

BBQ ribs,
American-style

There are all sorts of pretentious foodie words you could use to describe this dish, but essentially it is just plain yummy. A very hungry bloke could just about demolish this amount all by himself, though it could stretch four ways in polite company.

The secret to moist, tender ribs is the two-step cooking process: either slow-roasting or slow-braising the ribs first; then finishing them off on the barbie. It takes a bit of work, but the results are worth it.

4 whole racks (about 5 kg) American-style
pork spare ribs, cut in half lengthways
(ask your butcher to do this for you)

MARINADE
1 tablespoon ground paprika
½ teaspoon ground cayenne pepper
½ teaspoon red chilli flakes
½ teaspoon celery salt
¼ teaspoon garlic powder
¼ teaspoon onion powder
1 teaspoon sea salt
½ teaspoon freshly ground black pepper
½ cup lemon juice
½ cup Worcestershire sauce
1½ cups cider vinegar

SPICY BARBECUE SAUCE
2 cups tomato sauce
½ cup water
2 tablespoons brown sugar
¼ teaspoon ground cayenne pepper
2 tablespoons Worcestershire sauce
⅓ cup cider vinegar
1 tablespoon lemon juice
1 teaspoon mustard powder

Mix all the marinade ingredients together and spread over the ribs in a large baking dish. Cover with plastic film and refrigerate for 2–12 hours. Bring the meat to room temperature by removing from the fridge half an hour before cooking. Retain the marinade for basting.

Preheat the oven to 180°C and roast the ribs for 2 hours, basting every half an hour with the reserved marinade, then set them aside to cool. (The ribs can be marinated and roasted ahead of time – either on the morning of your barbie or even the day before.)

To prepare the barbecue sauce, place all the ingredients in a deep saucepan, stir well until combined and bring to the boil, then simmer for 5 minutes. Keep the sauce warm until you're ready to serve.

Preheat your flat grillplate to very hot and smoking, and brown the ribs on both sides for a minute or so. Brush plenty of barbecue sauce over the ribs and cook for a minute more on each side.

Pour the remaining warm sauce over the ribs and serve.

Serves 4 – or just the author on a good day

Veal cutlets with capsicum and balsamic vinegar

Here's another 1980s bistro fave that is still delicious, looks fantastic, and is all of 10 minutes work start to finish, which makes it a great school-night recipe.

The secret to this dish is buying the best-quality veal you can get your hands on.

4 veal cutlets, each 1.5–2 cm thick
½ cup good-quality extra virgin olive oil
3 capsicums (1 green, 1 red, 1 yellow), white insides and seeds removed, cut into 2 cm strips
sea salt and freshly ground black pepper, to taste
½ cup shredded basil or oregano leaves
⅓ cup good-quality balsamic vinegar

Rub the veal cutlets with 1 tablespoon of the oil, and the capsicum strips with another.

Season the meat with salt and pepper and place on a preheated flat grillplate or chargrill, along with the capsicum.

Cook the meat until done to your liking, turning once during cooking. Turn the capsicum as frequently as required to stop it burning. Rest the meat, loosely covered in foil, for 5 minutes before serving.

Mix the basil or oregano and the cooked capsicum together in a bowl. Place a veal cutlet and some capsicum on each serving plate, pouring over the juices from the resting meat.

Drizzle the remaining olive oil and the balsamic vinegar over the top, and serve.

Serves 4

Korean minute steaks

There's no end to the flavours from around the world that you can add to barbecued meat. While the ingredients used here are all quite commonplace, their combination produces a very distinctive taste. This is a simple marinade that adds lots of oomph to a nice piece of steak.

4 slices beef scotch fillet, each about 1 cm thick
2 large cloves garlic, crushed
¼ cup light soy sauce
1 tablespoon sesame oil
1 tablespoon castor sugar
1 tablespoon neutral oil (see page 10)

Pound each piece of steak with a meat mallet or rolling pin until half its original thickness.

Combine the rest of the ingredients together with the steaks in a shallow dish and marinate, covered with plastic film, in the fridge for 2–12 hours.

Bring the meat to room temperature by removing from the fridge half an hour before cooking. Cook the marinated steak on a preheated chargrill over high heat for just a minute or two on each side.

Serve with kimchi (Korean cabbage pickles), available from specialty Asian food shops, or some crusty bread to soak up the delicious juices.

Serves 4

Milk-fed veal with asparagus and fresh herbs

We're into the gourmet end of the barbecue repertoire with this dish, but it's remarkably simple. You chargrill some veggies, chop some fresh herbs and make a nice sharp vinaigrette, and then, finally, quickly sear the veal. The only trick is in finding really good-quality veal (the lovely pale milk-fed stuff is pretty hard to get, but a good butcher should be able to help).

8 large thin slices milk-fed veal (60–70 g each)
⅔ cup extra virgin olive oil
2 tablespoons pine nuts
12 broad beans, shelled
1 bunch asparagus, ends discarded,
   sliced lengthways
4 baby zucchini, sliced lengthways
20 basil leaves, thinly sliced
20 mint leaves, thinly sliced
3 tablespoons lemon juice
sea salt and freshly ground black pepper, to taste

Remove the veal from the fridge half an hour before cooking to bring to room temperature, and place in a shallow dish. Coat with 1 tablespoon of the oil then set aside.

Lightly toast the pine nuts in a dry non-stick frying pan for a couple of minutes until browned, then set aside to cool. Keep an eye on them – they can go from golden brown to burnt in a matter of seconds.

In a small saucepan, bring some water to the boil and add the broad beans, cooking for 30 seconds. Drain them and leave to cool for a few minutes, then remove the tough outer skins.

Preheat the chargrill to hot, brush the asparagus and zucchini with another tablespoon of oil then grill over high heat for about 2 minutes, turning to cook evenly. Once charred, transfer to a large bowl and add the beans, pine nuts, herbs, lemon juice, salt, pepper and the remaining oil, and stir to combine.

Place the veal on the hot grill and cook for 30–60 seconds each side (this will depend on the thickness of the meat – you want it charred on the outside but still pink and tender on the inside).

To serve, place two slices of veal on each plate, scatter the asparagus mixture over the top, and drizzle over any remaining dressing from the bowl.

Serves 4

Milk-fed veal with
asparagus and fresh herbs

Jerk beef brisket

A jerk is not only the mate who feels up your wife or girlfriend at your barbecue – it's also one of the most popular types of Caribbean cooking. There are as many different jerk recipes as there are American rib variations, but your basic jerk should always consist of thyme, garlic, allspice and Scotch bonnet chillies. And, not surprisingly, given the chillies, jerk should kick like a mule. Jerk marinades work wonderfully with pork legs or shoulders, whole chickens (or wings for snacks), and beef cuts like brisket that are best slow-cooked.

1.5–2 kg beef brisket,
   trimmed of excess fat

JERK MARINADE
6 cloves garlic
1 bunch spring onions,
   trimmed and roughly chopped
2 tablespoons allspice
1 teaspoon cinnamon
1 teaspoon nutmeg
1 tablespoon dried thyme *or* 2 tablespoons
   fresh thyme leaves
1 teaspoon freshly ground black pepper
1 tablespoon celery salt
6 Scotch bonnet chillies or medium
   red chillies (seeds and all for this)
½ cup neutral oil (see page 10)

Process all the marinade ingredients in a food processor or blender until a smooth paste forms. Add a little more oil if it is too dry.

Rub the paste all over the meat (or better still, make the jerk that was feeling up your wife or girlfriend do it), then cover and marinate in the fridge for 2–12 hours.

Bring the meat to room temperature by removing from the fridge half an hour before cooking. Place the meat on a rack in the middle of your barbecue, and cook, covered, on a low–medium heat for 3 hours, making sure the heat is surrounding the meat on both sides but is not directly underneath.

Slice and serve on crusty bread with rocket and lime wedges, and lots of icy cold beer.

Serves 6–8

Thai beef salad

This poor dish has been bastardised by more third-rate 'chefs' than almost any other. At its best it is a rich, lively, beautifully balanced dish – the classic Thai contrast of hot, sour, sweet and salty. At its worst, it is anonymous, vaguely Asian-tasting nothingness.

For your guests' sake, it's worth buying fresh ingredients and making the real McCoy.

Palm sugar is available in some large supermarkets with special Asian sections, or in any Asian food store.

1 tablespoon long-grain or jasmine rice
100 g rice vermicelli noodles
2 sirloin steaks, each 2–3 cm thick
1 red onion *or* 2 shallots, peeled and finely sliced
1 bunch fresh mint, leaves picked
2 bunches fresh coriander, leaves picked
10 cherry tomatoes, cut in half
2 tablespoons roughly ground unsalted peanuts

DRESSING
½ cup lime juice
⅓ cup fish sauce
1 teaspoon grated palm sugar
2 cloves garlic, crushed
1 medium red chilli, de-seeded and sliced

Place the rice in a small frying pan and cook until lightly golden. Allow to cool, then grind to a crunchy powder consistency using a mortar and pestle.

Place the noodles in a bowl of very hot water for 5 minutes, then drain well.

Briefly cook the steaks on a preheated chargrill until they are just rare – take care not to overcook them. Set them aside to rest until they are almost cooled, then cut off any fat and gristle, and slice into 0.5–1 cm slices.

Place the noodles in a serving bowl with the onion or shallots, fresh herbs, tomatoes and ground rice. Add the slices of meat to the bowl and toss through.

Mix all the dressing ingredients together until the palm sugar dissolves. Taste and make sure the sweet, sour, salty and hot components are to your liking.

Pour the dressing over the salad, sprinkle the peanuts over the top, and serve.

Serves 4 as a light meal

The mixed gorilla

These days, with everyone telling us what we can and can't do, one of the simple pleasures in life has all but disappeared – the mixed grill. For generations the mixed gorilla was the standard fare of country cafés (before they were replaced by fast-food chains) and pubs (before they had dining rooms and $30+ mains).

If you don't fancy offal, skip the liver and kidney and shout yourself another lamb cutlet. Be proud! Pile that meat high! Don't let anyone stop you – every man deserves a mixed gorilla once in a while.

This version feeds one hungry bloke, but just multiply everything by four to feed a group.

1 fillet steak, about 1.5 cm thick

1 lamb cutlet

1 kidney, cut in half, white core removed

1 small slice calf's liver

3–4 tablespoons olive oil

salt and freshly ground black pepper, to taste

1 beef sausage

1 bacon rasher

1 small ripe tomato, cut in half

1 egg, optional

1 tablespoon grain or Australian
    mustard, to serve

Lightly coat the steak, lamb cutlet, kidney and liver with the oil and season well with salt and pepper. Grill all the meats, the offal and the tomato on a preheated chargrill until done to your liking (the sausage will take the longest, so start with that).

Fry the egg on the flat grillplate or in a frying pan.

Pile the whole lot onto your plate, and serve the mustard on the side. You might as well go the whole hog and have it with chips and doughy white bread and butter.

Serves 1

Beef short ribs

Ribs are perfect for the barbecue, and by braising them for an hour or so beforehand you'll get a much more tender result. While sweet, sticky pork ribs are the norm in Australia, these meatier, spicy beef ribs are seriously underrated.

To get a bit of a head start, the marinating and braising stages can be done the day before or the morning of your barbecue.

1.5–2 kg beef short ribs, cut into individual
  ribs (ask your butcher to do this for you)
3 cloves garlic, crushed
1 tablespoon neutral oil (see page 10)
1 cup tomato sauce
2 tablespoons tomato paste
2 tablespoons Worcestershire sauce
½ cup cider vinegar
1 × 375 ml can beer
⅓ cup honey

SPICE RUB
1 teaspoon onion powder
1 teaspoon garlic powder
1 teaspoon ground coriander
2 teaspoons dry mustard
½ teaspoon ground cloves
½ teaspoon cayenne pepper
1 teaspoon ground chilli

Mix the spice rub ingredients together in a clean, dry plastic bag. Place the ribs in the bag, tie up the top and shake thoroughly to coat. Leave in the bag and refrigerate for 4–12 hours.

In a large saucepan or stockpot, soften the garlic in the oil without browning it. Add all the remaining ingredients and stir together to combine.

Add the beef ribs to the pan and top with just enough water to cover them. Bring the pan to the boil then simmer very gently over low heat for 1½ hours.

Remove the braised ribs from the pan and set aside. Increase the heat to high and reduce the braising liquid down to 1–2 cups.

Cook the ribs on a preheated flat grillplate until caramelised but not black, basting regularly with the reduced braising liquid. Pour the remaining liquid over the ribs to serve.

Serves 4–6

Simon and Garfunkel steak

Those over 40 or so might remember Simon and Garfunkel's song 'Scarborough Fair' from the movie *The Graduate* with Dustin Hoffman and Anne Bancroft, with the famous line about parsley, sage, rosemary and thyme. This recipe uses those herbs on a beef fillet, hence the Simon and Garfunkel bit. It tastes great and it's dead easy to make.

2 tablespoons olive oil
2 tablespoons each dried parsley, sage,
  rosemary and thyme
1 teaspoon salt
½ teaspoon freshly ground black pepper
4 slices beef fillet, each about 5 cm thick

Arrange two plates beside each other, one containing the oil, the other with the dried parsley, sage, rosemary, thyme, salt and pepper mixed together.

Pat the steaks dry with kitchen paper, then roll the sides of each one in the oil and then in the herb mixture, to achieve a nice herb crust around the edge of each steak.

Cook the steaks on a preheated flat grillplate for a few minutes on each side, until done to your liking, then set them aside to rest, loosely covered with foil, for a couple of minutes before serving with a salad.

Serves 4

Simon and
Garfunkel steak

The new filet mignon

The new filet mignon

Filet mignon, a thick piece of beef eye fillet wrapped in a slice of bacon, was oh-so-chic throughout the 1960s, '70s and '80s. A flash dinner out more often than not featured this ubiquitous dish, and there wasn't much wrong with it – except that all you could taste was the salty bacon, which completely smothered the flavour of the beef.

A few decades on and this smarter version uses a very thin slice of prosciutto, which adds just a little saltiness without overwhelming the taste buds.

4 thin slices prosciutto
4 pieces beef eye fillet, each about 5 cm thick
1 clove garlic, cut in half
1 tablespoon olive oil
freshly ground black pepper, to taste
a drizzle of good-quality extra virgin olive oil, to serve
a splash of good-quality balsamic vinegar, to serve

Wrap a slice of prosciutto around each piece of steak and secure with a toothpick if necessary.

Rub each end of the steaks with the cut garlic, then brush with olive oil and season with black pepper. Cook on a preheated flat grillplate or chargrill over a medium–high heat, until done to your liking.

Set the steaks aside to rest, loosely covered with foil, for a couple of minutes before drizzling a few drops of extra virgin olive oil and balsamic vinegar over each. Serve with some crusty bread and rocket.

Serves 4

Slow-cooked beef brisket

For this dish, you'll need a barbecue big enough to have heat either side of the baking dish but not directly underneath it – a six-burner is ideal. Of course, you'll also need a lid to cover the dish while it cooks – if you don't have one that fits your baking dish, close the hood of the barbie instead.

sea salt and freshly ground black pepper
(about a tablespoon of each)
1.5–2 kg beef brisket, trimmed of excess fat
⅓ cup olive oil
2 large red onions, sliced
4 cloves garlic, sliced
2 tablespoons finely grated orange zest
1 tablespoon paprika
1 tablespoon dried oregano
2 × 400 g cans good-quality Italian tomatoes,
coarsely chopped
2 cups homemade chicken stock,
***or* 1 cup ready-made chicken or veal stock,**
diluted with 1 cup water
4 bay leaves
½ cup fresh oregano leaves, finely sliced

Sprinkle the salt and pepper all over the meat. Using the baking dish of your barbecue over a direct flame, brown the meat in the oil over medium heat for just a minute or two either side.

Remove the meat and set aside. Add the onions, garlic and orange zest to the baking dish, cooking for just a minute to soften the onion. Stir through the paprika and dried oregano, then return the meat to the pan, making sure it is coated in the onion mixture on both sides.

Add the tomatoes, stock and bay leaves and bring to the boil before turning off the heat directly under the baking dish, and turning the heat on either side to low. Cook for 3 hours with the lid on, checking occasionally to make sure the dish is not drying out – if you find it is, add a small amount of water. After 3 hours, take off the lid and cook for a further 1 hour uncovered.

Once cooked, remove the meat from the pan and slice on a chopping board. Return it to the pan, adding the fresh oregano, then cover and set aside to rest for 10–20 minutes. Check the seasoning before serving.

Serve with mashed potatoes, pasta or couscous, or as a filling for a white bread roll.

Serves 6–8

Chinese pork ribs

Master-stock cooking is the basis of a lot of the Chinese food that we enjoy (it's the secret behind the delicious, tender flesh of crispy-skin chicken). Meat is gently poached in a rich, slightly sweet stock to infuse it with aromatic flavours. Here we shorten this poaching process and then grill the ribs to finish off. And there is an optional sweet sticky sauce to go on top, for a classic Chinese-restaurant taste. Your local Asian food shop will have the more hard-to-find ingredients.

2 whole racks (about 2.5 kg) American-style
 pork spare ribs, cut into four-rib sections
 (ask your butcher to do this for you)
neutral oil (see page 10), for brushing

MASTER STOCK
1 clove garlic, sliced
1 knob ginger (3 cm long), roughly chopped
2 sticks cinnamon or cassia bark
1 piece orange peel (about 4 cm × 2 cm),
 white pith removed *or* a piece of dried
 orange or tangerine peel
100 g palm sugar
200 ml mirin or Shaohsing rice wine
100 ml dark soy sauce
1 litre cold water

SWEET STICKY SAUCE (OPTIONAL)
⅔ cup plum sauce
⅓ cup Chinese barbecue sauce
1 teaspoon finely grated orange zest
½ cup cold water

Place all the master stock ingredients in a large stockpot, then bring to the boil and simmer very gently for half an hour. Remove the ribs and set them aside to rest for 20 minutes.

To make the sweet sticky sauce, mix the plum and barbecue sauces in a small saucepan with the orange zest and water and bring to the boil. Simmer for 1 minute.

Brush the ribs with a little neutral oil and cook on a pre-heated flat grillplate, until just slightly charred and crispy.

Pour the sweet sticky sauce over the ribs as you serve.

Serves 4

Beef fillet with garlic and herb prawns

Here's everyone's favourite entrée and main course combined in the same dish. Surf 'n' turf is pretty daggy, but it's a great combination of flavours and textures – and we're barbecuing, so who cares about being daggy?

16 medium green (raw) king prawns
4 pieces beef eye fillet, each about 3 cm thick
1 tablespoon olive oil
sea salt and freshly ground black pepper, to taste
4 tablespoons butter
⅓ cup extra virgin olive oil
2 cloves garlic, crushed
½ cup fresh oregano leaves _or_ 1 teaspoon dried oregano
½ cup flat-leaf parsley leaves, roughly chopped
½ cup finely chopped chives

To prepare the prawns, twist off the head and, with a sharp knife, make a 5 mm-deep cut through the back of the shell. Pull out the dark intestinal vein and peel off the shell, leaving on the last section of tail if desired.

Rub the beef fillets with the tablespoon of olive oil and season well with salt and pepper.

Cook the fillets on a preheated flat grillplate until medium–rare or done to your liking. Set aside to rest, loosely covered with foil, for about 5 minutes.

While the meat is resting, melt the butter in the extra virgin olive oil in your wok over the highest flame, then add the prawns, garlic and herbs. Season well with some salt and pepper. Cook until the prawns are firm to the touch and opaque.

To serve, place a piece of beef on each plate and spoon the prawn mixture over the top. Serve with some crusty bread to mop up the garlic butter. A sharply dressed green salad goes really well with this dish.

Serves 4

Steak with anchovy butter

Legendary chef Damien Pignolet has served a to-die-for Café de Paris butter at Sydney's Bistro Moncur since the doors opened over a dozen years ago. The upside of this dish is that it tastes wonderfully complex, the downside is that it's painfully complex to make, with 25 different ingredients (one of which is anchovies).

This recipe doesn't pretend to be even a simplified version of this classic, but it is a nice way to tart up a steak (and one of the ingredients is anchovies).

1 tablespoon olive oil
4 pieces T-bone, sirloin, fillet or rump steak,
    each about 2 cm thick

ANCHOVY BUTTER
100 g butter, softened
6 anchovy fillets in oil, drained and very finely chopped
1 teaspoon capers, drained
1 teaspoon very finely chopped flat-leaf parsley
1 small clove garlic, crushed
½ teaspoon dried rosemary
½ teaspoon tomato sauce
1 teaspoon lemon juice
sea salt and freshly ground black pepper, to taste

To make the butter, mix all the ingredients in a small bowl, pressing them together with the back of a fork, then transfer the butter to a sheet of greaseproof paper. Roll into a sausage shape about the diameter of a 20-cent piece and twist both ends to seal. Refrigerate and cut into discs as required. (It should keep for about a week in the fridge or for several months in the freezer – wrap in a layer of plastic film before freezing.)

Rub the oil all over the steaks, season with salt and pepper and cook them on a preheated flat grillplate or chargrill until done to your liking.

Place a disc of the anchovy butter on top of each steak and serve immediately with roasted new potatoes.

Serves 4

On the lamb

Lamb with red wine and thyme

Some people are frightened of marinating; they worry that the flavours will be too overpowering. A little commonsense is required here. A delicate veal scallopini or a small white fish like John Dory hardly needs to sit in a strongly flavoured marinade for days. However, a large leg of lamb like this or a big hunk of beef can really benefit from some serious marinating to enhance the flavours.

1 large boned leg of lamb (about 2 kg),
   trimmed of excess fat and butterflied
   (ask your butcher to do this for you)

MARINADE
2 cloves garlic, crushed
1 onion, very thinly sliced
1 large carrot, thinly sliced
2 teaspoons dried thyme leaves
4 bay leaves
1 teaspoon freshly ground black pepper
400 ml red wine
200 ml red wine vinegar
100 ml olive oil

Mix all the marinade ingredients together in a shallow dish. Place the lamb in the dish and coat with the marinade, then cover with plastic film and marinate in the fridge for 12 hours.

Alternatively, you can mix all the marinade ingredients together with the lamb in a plastic bag (make sure there are no holes in it), tie up the top, then use your fingers to massage the liquid into every bit of the lamb through the plastic. Marinate in the fridge for 12 hours.

Bring the meat to room temperature by removing from the fridge 1 hour before cooking. Immediately before cooking, remove the meat from the marinade and pat dry with kitchen paper.

Place on a preheated hot flat grillplate and cook for 5 minutes, then turn the meat over and reduce the heat to medium. Close the hood of the barbecue and cook for 20 minutes or until done to your liking.

Once cooked, remove the lamb from the grill and set aside to rest, loosely covered with foil, for 15 minutes.

Serve with roast or boiled potatoes and a sharply dressed salad.

Serves 6

Moroccan lamb chops

Easy peasy lemon squeezy. Here's a dish that takes 2 minutes to prepare before you go to work in the morning, and all that's left to do when you get home is to throw the meat on a hot barbie.

8 lamb chump or loin chops *or* 12–16 lamb cutlets
2 tablespoons ready-made Moroccan seasoning
1 teaspoon sea salt
⅓ cup olive oil
2 tablespoons lemon juice
2 tablespoons finely chopped flat-leaf parsley

Mix all the ingredients together in a shallow dish and cover with plastic film (or you can be really lazy and squish everything together in the plastic bag the lamb came in). Marinate in the fridge for 2–12 hours.

Bring the meat to room temperature by removing from the fridge half an hour before cooking.

Cook the chops on a preheated flat grillplate for about 2 minutes each side, then finish on the chargrill for another couple of minutes each side to allow the fat to drain away. Serve immediately.

Serves 4

Moroccan lamb chops

Baharat lamb chops

Baharat is a Middle Eastern spice blend (in fact, the word *baharat* literally translates as 'spices'). There are a squillion different variations of ingredients, but it is essentially a mix of dry spices used to marinate meat or vegetables, or to flavour stews. Here it's used to jazz up an economical cut of meat – the humble lamb chop.

(You can also use baharat to spice up your roast spuds. Take one quantity of baharat spice rub, mix it with olive oil and plenty of sea salt, rub over small new potatoes cut into halves, and roast them in a 200°C oven for about 45 minutes.)

8 lamb chops (chump, loin or cutlets)
2 tablespoons olive oil
sea salt, to taste
lemon wedges, to garnish

BAHARAT SPICE RUB
2 tablespoons sweet paprika
1 tablespoon ground cumin
1 teaspoon ground cinnamon
1 teaspoon ground coriander
1 teaspoon ground cloves
1 teaspoon ground cardamom
1 teaspoon freshly ground black pepper
½ teaspoon ground star anise
½ teaspoon ground nutmeg
juice and finely grated zest of one lemon

Mix the spice rub ingredients together, add the olive oil, and rub into the lamb chops. Place in a shallow dish, cover with plastic film and marinate in the fridge for 2–12 hours.

Bring the meat to room temperature by removing from the fridge half an hour before cooking. Season with salt, cook on a preheated flat grillplate for about 4 minutes on each side, then finish off on the chargrill for another minute or so each side, to allow the fat to drain away.

Garnish with lemon wedges and serve with a green salad.

Serves 4

Lemony, herby lamb loins

Lamb loins are a luxurious sort of cut and very lean when the outer layer of fat is removed. In this case, though, ask your butcher to leave the fat on, as when it's seared on a hot grill, the delicious flavours are released and absorbed into the meat – yummo! (Your fat-free, politically correct friends can cut the fat off later if they like.)

2 lamb loins (about 200 g each),
**   outer layer of fat left on**

MARINADE
2 teaspoons finely grated lemon zest
1 teaspoon lemon juice
½ teaspoon freshly ground black pepper
1 teaspoon dried rosemary
1 teaspoon ground cumin
1 teaspoon sea salt

Combine all the marinade ingredients in a shallow dish and add the loins, cover with plastic film and marinate in the fridge for 2 hours. Bring the meat to room temperature by removing from the fridge half an hour before cooking.

Preheat your flat grillplate to hot and sear the meat, fat-side down, for about 3–4 minutes, then turn and cook the other side for 2 minutes.

Once cooked, remove the meat from the grill and set aside to rest, loosely covered with foil, for a few minutes before slicing and serving.

Serves 4–6

Lemony,
herby lamb loins

Six-hour lamb salad

This really slow-cooked dry-rubbed lamb is delicious served traditionally with baked vegetables, but lighter and just as yummy with this Mediterranean salad.

2 teaspoons celery salt

2 teaspoons ground coriander

1½ teaspoons ground cumin

1 lamb shoulder (about 1.5 kg)

1 bunch baby beetroot, stems and leaves discarded

sea salt and freshly ground black pepper, to taste

600 g butternut pumpkin, cut into 2 cm pieces

1 tablespoon neutral oil (see page 10)

1 punnet cherry tomatoes, cut into halves

2 teaspoons dried thyme

1 large handful baby rocket

1 medium red onion, finely sliced

½ cup shelled pistachios

½ cup extra virgin olive oil

¼ cup good-quality balsamic vinegar

In a large bowl, mix the celery salt, coriander and cumin together. Add lamb and rub the spiced salt all over the lamb. Cover with plastic film and refrigerate for 4–12 hours.

Preheat the oven to 180°C. Wrap each beetroot in foil, seasoning with salt and pepper before sealing, and place in a roasting dish. In a separate roasting dish, coat the pumpkin pieces in the oil. Roast the pumpkin and beetroot for 40 minutes.

Halfway through the cooking time, place the tomatoes in a separate small roasting dish, sprinkle over the thyme and some salt, and roast for 20 minutes.

When the beetroot is cool enough to handle, rub the skins off with your fingers – plastic disposable gloves are a good idea if you don't want to have purple hands for days. Chop the peeled beetroot into small wedges.

Bring the meat to room temperature by removing from the fridge half an hour before cooking. Place the lamb on a rack in the baking dish of your barbecue. Fill the dish with 2 cups of water and cover the whole lot loosely with foil. Cook for 5–6 hours with the barbecue hood closed, making sure the heat is surrounding the meat on both sides but is not directly underneath. Do not let the dish dry out – check now and then to see if the water needs topping up. Remove the foil for the last hour of cooking.

Once cooked, remove the lamb from the barbecue and set aside to rest, loosely covered with foil, for 20 minutes while you assemble the salad.

Arrange the rocket in a large serving dish and top with the roasted pumpkin, beetroot and the onion. Roughly shred the lamb with two forks and add to the salad, then scatter over the roasted tomatoes and pistachios. Mix the olive oil and balsamic vinegar together, season with salt and pepper, and pour over the salad. Serve immediately.

Serves 4–6

Greek lamb with oregano

Greeks do like their lamb – and they're pretty partial to some oregano to go with it. Slow-cooking a leg of lamb in oil and water will get it fall-apart tender, and the flavour will be strong and uncomplicated.

1 boned leg of lamb (about 1.2 kg), butterflied
    (ask your butcher to do this for you)
⅓ cup olive oil
juice of one lemon
1 dessertspoon sea salt
3 cloves garlic, crushed
2 tablespoons dried oregano

Place the lamb in the baking dish of your barbecue. Mix together the oil, lemon juice, salt and garlic and spread evenly over both sides of the lamb. Sprinkle the oregano over both sides and add enough cold water to the dish so that it just covers the lamb.

Place a sheet of baking paper or foil over the top of the lamb, tucking it in around the sides of the dish to seal and keep the moisture in.

Cook on low heat for 2½ hours, making sure the heat is surrounding the lamb on both sides but is not directly underneath.

Once cooked, remove the baking dish from the barbecue and set aside to rest, still covered, for 10 minutes.

Slice the lamb, then serve with the roasting juices and some roast vegetables or a salad.

Serves 6

Sweet sticky lamb cutlets

The rules have changed when it comes to cooking Chinese – now there are no rules.

These chargrilled lamb cutlets are hardly the fare of old-fashioned Cantonese takeaways. They are a modern Asian, East-meets-West sort of thing, and take just a couple of minutes on the wok and chargrill.

12 lamb cutlets, 'restaurant cut' and trimmed
    of fat (ask your butcher to do this for you)
2 tablespoons neutral oil (see page 10)
1 teaspoon finely chopped ginger
1 clove garlic, finely chopped
4 cups fresh bean sprouts
½ cup finely chopped spring onions
    (dark green part only)
2 tablespoons hoisin sauce

MARINADE
2 tablespoons hoisin sauce
1 teaspoon sesame oil
1 teaspoon soy sauce

Mix the marinade ingredients in a large bowl and add the lamb, stirring to coat all the meat. Cover with plastic film and marinate in the fridge for 2 hours.

Bring the meat to room temperature by removing from the fridge half an hour before cooking.

On a preheated chargrill, cook the lamb cutlets until medium–rare or done to your liking, then remove them from the grill and set aside to rest, loosely covered with foil, while you cook the vegetables.

Heat the wok to very hot, then add the oil. Once the oil is hot, add the ginger, garlic, bean sprouts and spring onion. Stir-fry for 30 seconds or so, then add the hoisin sauce and stir-fry for a further 30 seconds or so.

Arrange the vegetables on four serving plates and place three lamb cutlets on each, pouring over any juices from the resting meat.

Serves 4

Sweet sticky lamb cutlets

Quick Asian
lamb cutlets

This is a no-fuss recipe with plenty of flavour. The kecap manis adds both saltiness and sweetness, but you'll need to flatten the cutlets out to reduce the cooking time or the sugar in the sauce will burn (trust the voice of charred-cutlet experience).

These cutlets also work well as finger food.

12 lamb cutlets, trimmed of excess fat
⅓ cup kecap manis
3 cloves garlic, crushed
2 tablespoons mirin or Chinese rice wine
1 tablespoon finely chopped coriander leaves

Pound the lamb cutlets with a meat mallet or rolling pin to a thickness of about 5 mm.

Combine all the remaining ingredients in a shallow dish, add the cutlets, then cover with plastic film and marinate in the fridge for 4–12 hours. Bring the meat to room temperature by removing from the fridge half an hour before cooking.

Preheat your chargrill to hot, and cook the cutlets for a minute or so either side until the outsides are caramelised but the insides are still pink.

Serve with stir-fried vegetables.

Serves 4

Mint-marinated lamb
cutlets with zucchini

There's something really comforting about the combination of lamb and mint. The sweetness of mint seems to work so much better with lamb than with any other type of meat. This is a really straightforward dish that adults and kids alike will love, but if it doesn't need to be kid-friendly, try adding a big pinch of dried chilli flakes to the marinade for some bite.

12 lamb cutlets
6 small zucchini, cut in half lengthways
lemon wedges, to garnish

MARINADE
1 tablespoon dried mint
½ cup olive oil
¼ cup lemon juice
1 teaspoon sea salt
½ teaspoon freshly ground black pepper

Combine all the marinade ingredients together in a shallow dish, then add the meat, making sure that all the cutlets are well coated. Cover with plastic film and marinate in the fridge for 2 hours. Bring the meat to room temperature by removing from the fridge half an hour before cooking.

Cook the lamb cutlets on a preheated chargrill for just a few minutes each side until done to your liking. Add the zucchini to the chargrill halfway through cooking the lamb.

Once cooked, remove the lamb and zucchini from the grill and set aside to rest, loosely covered with foil, for another couple of minutes.

Divide the zucchini between four plates and top with the lamb cutlets. Garnish with lemon wedges and serve immediately.

Serves 4

Mint-marinated lamb
cutlets with zucchini

'Crying' lamb with spring vegetables

The idea of cooking meat over vegetables and letting the juices drip down into them has been around since Pontius was a pilot. At the chicken rotisserie stalls of St Tropez a dozen chickens rotate in rows, and all the lovely cooking juices flavour the bed of provençale vegetables, grapes and olives underneath.

This technique works equally well with a young leg of lamb with beautiful spring vegetables underneath, and plenty of fresh herbs added at the last minute.

1 small leg of lamb (about 1.5 kg)
2 sprigs rosemary
4 cloves garlic (2 cloves finely sliced,
    2 cloves cut into matchsticks)
sea salt and freshly ground black pepper, to taste
2 capsicums (1 red and 1 green),
    white insides and seeds removed
2 medium red onions
6 ripe roma tomatoes
1 small eggplant
4 medium or 2 large zucchini
6 new potatoes, cut in half (optional)
20 small black olives
⅓ cup extra virgin olive oil
20 basil leaves, torn
1 cup flat-leaf parsley leaves

Make about eight 2 cm-deep incisions in the top of the lamb leg, and force four rosemary leaves and a garlic matchstick into each. Season the leg well with sea salt and freshly ground black pepper.

Chop the capsicums, onions, tomatoes, eggplant and zucchini into even pieces (around 3 cm). Place in the baking dish of your barbecue with the potatoes (if using), the sliced garlic, olives and two tablespoons of the oil.

If the dish has a rack, place the lamb on this; if not, place the lamb directly on top of the vegetables. Cook over low heat with the lid closed, ensuring the heat is not directly underneath the meat but surrounding it on both sides. Check the meat after about an hour to see if it's cooked – if not, give it another 15 minutes.

Once the meat is cooked, remove the baking dish from the barbecue and set aside to rest, loosely covered with foil, for about 20 minutes.

Stir the basil and parsley and remaining oil through the vegetables just before serving.

Spoon plenty of vegetables and cooking juices onto warm serving plates, and serve with lamb slices on top.

Serves 4–6

Sesame-coated lamb cutlets

These are sticky and sweet and really tasty, and you could serve them either as a main course or as a delicious plate of (substantial) finger food for 12.

A word of warning – you'll need to keep the heat very low and watch these like a hawk while they're cooking, otherwise the sesame coating will burn.

12 lamb cutlets, trimmed of all fat
1 cup sesame seeds
¼ cup neutral oil (see page 10)
sea salt, to taste

MARINADE
4 cloves garlic, crushed
2 teaspoons sesame oil
2 tablespoons light soy sauce
2 tablespoons honey
2 tablespoons Shaohsing rice wine (optional)

Mix the marinade ingredients together in a shallow bowl and add the lamb cutlets, ensuring that they are completely coated in the mixture. Cover with plastic film and marinate in the fridge for 2–12 hours.

Bring the meat to room temperature by removing from the fridge half an hour before cooking. Place the sesame seeds on a plate and roll the lamb cutlets around in them to cover.

Pour the oil over a preheated flat grillplate and cook the cutlets over low heat until the meat is medium–rare and the sesame seeds are golden brown and slightly scorched. Sprinkle a little sea salt over the cutlets and serve.

Serves 4

Indian-spiced leg of lamb

Is this a traditional Indian dish? Not in a fit. Is it delicious? You betcha.

1 boned leg of lamb (about 1.2 kg), butterflied (ask your butcher to do this for you)
lime slices, to garnish

RAITA
1 clove garlic, crushed
8 mint leaves, very finely sliced
1 cup plain yoghurt
1 tablespoon lime juice
1 small ripe tomato, de-seeded and diced
½ cup diced red capsicum
½ cup diced red onion
½ cup peeled, de-seeded and diced cucumber

MARINADE
1 cup plain yoghurt
2 tablespoons garam masala
½ teaspoon cayenne pepper
1 teaspoon dried mint leaves
2 tablespoons lime juice
1 knob ginger (3 cm long), grated
3 cloves garlic, crushed
1 teaspoon sea salt

To prepare the raita, combine all the ingredients and store, covered in plastic film, in the fridge.

Put all the marinade ingredients in a food processor and blend to a smooth paste.

Place the lamb in a shallow dish and coat with the marinade, then cover with plastic film and marinate in the fridge for 2–12 hours. Bring the meat to room temperature by removing from the fridge half an hour before cooking.

Preheat a chargrill or flat grillplate to medium–high, then sear the marinated lamb for a couple of minutes on each side. Reduce the heat to low, close the lid of your barbecue, and cook for a further 15–20 minutes, or until the meat is tender to the touch. Remove the lamb and set aside to rest, loosely covered with foil, for 15–20 minutes. Then slice and serve with the raita and some rocket salad, and garnish with slices of lime.

Serves 6

Indian-spiced
leg of lamb

Spice-rubbed lamb with couscous salad

While this book clearly doesn't aim to be a weight-watcher's guide to the barbecue, this recipe is positively bursting with goodness – a winning combination of lean meat and a light, healthy salad.

If you can't find ras el hanout, just use any Moroccan spice blend instead.

4 lamb loins (about 130 g each), trimmed of all fat
sea salt and freshly ground black pepper, to taste

MARINADE
1 tablespoon honey
1 teaspoon ground cumin
1 teaspoon ground coriander
2 tablespoons lime juice
2 tablespoons olive oil
1 clove garlic, crushed
1 medium red chilli, de-seeded and very finely sliced

COUSCOUS SALAD
½ cup currants
½ cup orange juice
1 cup slivered almonds
½ cup pine nuts
2 cups instant couscous, cooked as per instructions on packet
4 spring onions (white and pale green parts only), finely sliced
1 tablespoon fresh thyme leaves
1 cup diced red capsicum
1 teaspoon finely grated orange zest
½ cup extra virgin olive oil
1 teaspoon ras el hanout spice mix
1 tablespoon finely chopped medium red chilli (optional)

Combine the marinade ingredients in a shallow dish and add the lamb loins, making sure they are completely coated with the marinade. Cover with plastic film and marinate in the fridge for 2–24 hours. Bring the lamb to room temperature by removing from the fridge half an hour before cooking.

For the couscous salad, soak the currants in the orange juice for 20–30 minutes. Toast the almonds and pine nuts by cooking them in a dry frying pan over high heat until they become golden brown. Be careful though – they'll burn in a heartbeat.

Combine the currants, orange juice, toasted nuts and all the remaining couscous ingredients in a large bowl, adding more oil and orange juice if necessary. Season well with salt and pepper.

Place the lamb loins on a preheated chargrill and cook for a few minutes each side. Remove them from the grill and set aside to rest, loosely covered with foil, for 5–10 minutes. Cut each lamb loin into four thick slices and serve with couscous salad.

Serves 4

The chicken or the fish

Pancetta-wrapped spatchcock with honey and thyme

This is a really easy chook dish, and the honey adds a delicious sweetness to the meat. Try Italian elderflower or lavender honey if you can find it, or any good-quality variety from your local markets. Adding the honey towards the end means it won't burn or blacken the bird's skin.

8 sprigs fresh thyme *or* 1 teaspoon dried thyme
4 small spatchcocks, cut in half along the breast bone
8 thin slices pancetta or prosciutto
4 tablespoons honey
freshly ground black pepper, to taste

Preheat the chargrill to medium. Place a sprig of fresh thyme or a pinch of dried thyme on each spatchcock half and wrap a slice of pancetta around each one.

Sear the spatchcock halves quickly on the grill for a minute or two either side. Reduce the heat to medium and close the hood of the barbecue, then cook for 10 minutes.

Open the hood and drizzle the honey over the spatchcock halves, then close and cook for a few more minutes, or until the juices run clear when the point of a knife is inserted into the thickest part of the bird.

Grind a little black pepper over the top and serve with mashed potato, celeriac or parsnips.

Serves 4

Peri-peri little chooks

Of course you can use ready-made peri-peri sauce from the supermarket for this and you will get a fine result, but it will be even better if you make it from scratch.

Quail works just as well here in place of the spatchcock if you want to be a bit more adventurous and make a bit more mess.

Pretend you're still playing footy and serve these with chilled orange quarters to cool your mouth down – the traditional remedy for this hot little dish.

4 spatchcock, butterflied
(ask your butcher to do this for you)

PERI-PERI SAUCE
4 cloves garlic, chopped
2 teaspoons paprika
6 bird's-eye chillies, de-seeded and chopped
1 cup olive oil
2 teaspoons finely grated lime zest
2 tablespoons lime juice

Place all the sauce ingredients in a food processor and pulse a few times to combine. The sauce should be of a pouring consistency but not completely smooth.

Transfer the spatchcock to a shallow bowl and pour over half the sauce mixture, making sure that the birds are completely covered. Cover with plastic film and marinate for 2 hours in the fridge. Bring the spatchcock to room temperature by removing from the fridge half an hour before cooking.

Cook the spatchcock on a preheated chargrill over medium heat, basting them with the remaining sauce as you cook. They are cooked if the juices run clear when the point of a knife is inserted into the thickest part of the bird.

Set the spatchcock aside to rest, loosely covered with foil, for 5 minutes before serving.

Serves 4

Fresh herb chicken

Chicken fillets can sometimes be a bit bland and dry cooked on a barbecue, so try thighs instead of breasts, and add some moisture and flavour with this quick marinade.

This is a nice, light, almost healthy dish.

8 boneless chicken thigh fillets
  (about 140 g each), excess fat removed
lemon wedges, to garnish

MARINADE
½ cup olive oil
1 tablespoon lemon juice
2 cloves garlic, crushed
½ teaspoon freshly ground black pepper
½ teaspoon salt
1 tablespoon each fresh thyme, parsley
  and rosemary leaves, finely chopped

Combine all the marinade ingredients in a shallow bowl. Add the chicken thighs, making sure they are well coated with the marinade, cover with plastic film and marinate for 2 hours in the fridge. Bring the meat to room temperature by removing from the fridge half an hour before cooking.

Cook the chicken thighs on a preheated chargrill for a few minutes each side, or until the chicken is cooked through.

Garnish with lemon wedges and serve.

Serves 4

Texas drunken chicken

Also known as up-the-bum-chook, this dish is bound to get your guests talking. The chicken cooks on top of an opened can of beer, which makes the meat beautifully tender and tasty. You can buy specially designed and ridiculously expensive Texas drunken-chicken-holders from specialty barbecue stores, or you can just balance the chook on the beer can.

Important: make sure you remember to open the can of beer, or you'll be in all sorts of trouble!

1 medium organic or free-range chicken
 (about 1.7 kg)
1 × 375 ml can beer

GREAT AUSSIE BARBIE SPICE RUB
1 tablespoon sea salt
4 tablespoons celery salt
4 tablespoons ground paprika
1 tablespoon brown sugar
1 tablespoon mustard powder
1 tablespoon ground coriander
1 tablespoon freshly ground black pepper
½ tablespoon garlic powder
½ tablespoon onion powder
½ tablespoon dried thyme
½ tablespoon cayenne pepper

Mix all the spice rub ingredients together in a bowl. This will make about a cup – more than you need for this recipe, so transfer 2–3 tablespoons to a smaller bowl then store the rest in a tightly-sealed container (it will keep for months in the fridge).

Trim the chicken of any excess fat, especially from the breast or cavity, then rub the 2–3 tablespoons spice mix all over the chicken.

Open the can of beer and carefully lower the chicken onto it, then stand it, legs down, wings up, in the baking dish of your barbecue.

Place the baking dish in the middle of the barbecue with heat surrounding it on both sides, but not directly underneath. Close the hood and cook for 70–80 minutes. Check the chicken is cooked by inserting the point of a knife into the thickest part of the bird – the juices should run clear.

Once cooked, remove the chicken from the dish, carefully slide it off the beer can (it will be *very* hot), and set aside to rest, loosely covered with foil, for 10 minutes, then joint or carve and serve immediately. Discard the beer.

Serves 4

Tuna with tapenade and beans

Tuna works really well cooked on the barbecue, as it is dense and meaty and holds together nicely. A salty, garlicky tapenade is the perfect accompaniment. Don't buy the tapenade, make it yourself – it's all of 5 minutes work and the flavours will be so much more vibrant.

4 tuna steaks (about 150 g each), 2 cm thick
24 fresh green beans
olive oil, to rub over the fish
freshly ground black pepper, to taste
lemon wedges, to garnish

TAPENADE
2 cloves garlic, crushed
4 anchovy fillets in oil, drained
6 fresh basil leaves
1 cup pitted black Kalamata olives
about ½ cup extra virgin olive oil

Make sure the tuna is at room temperature by removing from the fridge half an hour before cooking.

To make the tapenade, combine the ingredients in a food processor, gradually adding enough olive oil to make a thick, smooth paste.

Preheat a flat grillplate or chargrill to very hot, rub a little oil over the tuna and sear for a minute on either side, leaving the centre quite rare. Remove the tuna from the grill and set aside to rest, loosely covered with foil, for up to 5 minutes.

Steam or boil the green beans and refresh in cold (preferably iced) water to maintain their colour and stop them cooking further, then set them aside.

Serve the tuna with the steamed or boiled beans alongside. Top the tuna with a spoonful of tapenade, some more extra virgin olive oil and freshly ground black pepper, and garnish with lemon wedges.

Serves 4

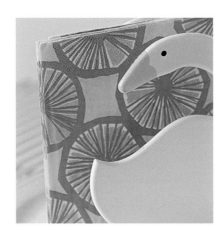

Chilli prawns on noodles

More and more people are wising up and using their barbecues for smelly, messy dishes like this to spare their kitchens the suffering. You can peel the prawns completely beforehand if you like, but half the fun is getting up to your elbows in the delicious sticky juices while trying to get the shells off. Jump in the pool afterwards to clean up.

Make sure you drain the noodles immediately prior to serving, or they will stick together and become a clumpy mess.

20 large green (raw) king prawns
2 tablespoons vegetable oil
2 cloves garlic, crushed
1 bird's-eye chilli, de-seeded and finely sliced,
    or more to taste
3 spring onions, trimmed and finely sliced
2 tablespoons chilli sauce
¼ cup tomato sauce
1 tablespoon soy sauce
1 teaspoon sugar
200 ml homemade chicken stock *or* 100 ml ready-made
    chicken stock, diluted with 100 ml water
2 teaspoons cornflour
1 × 250 g packet egg or wheat noodles
1 egg

To prepare the prawns, twist off the head and, with a sharp knife, make a 5 mm-deep cut through the back of the shell. Pull out the dark intestinal vein and peel off the shell, leaving on the last section of tail if desired.

Heat the oil in a wok and fry the prawns until they just turn pink, but are not cooked through. Remove from the wok and set aside.

Add the garlic, chilli and spring onions to the wok and fry for about 20 seconds, then add the chilli sauce, tomato sauce, soy sauce, sugar and chicken stock and simmer for 1 minute.

In a small cup or mug, blend the cornflour with a little water, then add this mixture to the wok and stir through. Return the prawns and their juices to the wok, and simmer for several minutes until the prawns are firm to the touch and opaque.

Cook the noodles as per the instructions on the packet.

Crack the egg into a small bowl and lightly beat, then stir briskly through the prawn mixture. Drain the cooked noodles, transfer to a plate and serve the prawns and sauce on top.

Serves 4

Swordfish with chunky caponata

Caponata is a lovely sweet-and-sour Italian vegetable salad that usually features as part of an antipasto spread. Here's a version with the vegetables cut into chunkier pieces than usual that is teamed with swordfish steaks.

½ cup neutral oil (see page 10)
1 large eggplant, cut into 2 cm cubes
⅓ cup olive oil
2 zucchini, cut into 2 cm chunks
1 large onion, cut into 2 cm chunks
2 ripe tomatoes, roughly chopped
1 celery heart, roughly chopped
4 large green olives, stones removed
1 heaped teaspoon salted capers, rinsed
6 basil leaves, finely sliced
¼ cup red wine vinegar
1 dessertspoon sugar
4 x 180 g swordfish steaks, about 1 cm thick
sea salt and freshly ground black pepper, to taste

In a large frying pan, heat the neutral oil, then add the eggplant and shallow-fry until browned. Remove with a slotted spoon and drain on kitchen paper.

Discard the neutral oil and add half the olive oil to the pan. Fry the zucchini until coloured on both sides. Remove and set aside, then add the remaining oil and soften the onion until it just starts to colour.

Add the tomatoes and celery and cook over medium heat for 5 minutes. Return the eggplant and zucchini to the pan and add all the other ingredients except the swordfish, cooking for just a minute to dissolve the sugar.

Brush the swordfish with a little olive oil and season well. Cook on a preheated chargrill over high heat for about a minute each side, until the fish is just cooked through.

Serve each swordfish steak with a generous spoonful of caponata.

Serves 4

Grilled tuna with niçoise salad

The purists find it hard to agree what really should go into a classic niçoise (it certainly has canned tuna). We're going to sidestep the issue by re-inventing the niçoise for the barbie, using fresh grilled tuna and adding some capers to sharpen up the dressing.

8 small new potatoes
4 eggs
24 fresh green beans
4 × 150–200 g tuna fillets
olive oil, for brushing
sea salt and freshly ground black pepper, to taste
4 very ripe medium-sized tomatoes, cut into
    six or eight pieces
about 12 cos lettuce leaves, cut across in
    4 cm-wide strips
about 20 small black olives
about 8 basil leaves, torn
8 anchovy fillets in oil, drained

DRESSING
½ cup extra virgin olive oil
2 tablespoons white wine vinegar
1 tablespoon lemon juice
sea salt and black pepper, to taste
½ teaspoon Dijon mustard
1 heaped teaspoon very finely chopped
    red shallot
1 clove garlic, crushed
1 heaped teaspoon capers,
    rinsed and finely chopped

Steam or boil the potatoes until just cooked, then cut in half and reserve. Hardboil the eggs and allow to cool, then peel and cut into quarters. Steam or boil the green beans and refresh in cold (preferably iced) water to maintain their colour and stop them cooking further.

Brush both sides of the tuna fillets with a little olive oil and season with sea salt and black pepper. Place on a preheated chargrill, turning just once until cooked to medium–rare. Remove from the grill and set aside to rest, loosely covered with foil, for 5 minutes while you make the dressing.

Mix all the dressing ingredients together in a small bowl. Divide the potatoes, eggs, beans, tomatoes, lettuce, olives, basil and anchovies evenly between four plates. Place a tuna fillet on top and then spoon over the dressing before serving.

Serves 4

Paella

This one's a challenge even for the more confident barbecuer. You'll find there are a few constants in all paella recipes: a flat-bottomed paella pan or very large flat frypan; smoked paprika; and Spanish calasparra rice, which is to paella what arborio rice is to risotto. After that, you can be a bit creative and add a combination of ingredients – chorizo, chicken, seafood, vegetables, and so on. If you can't get them in your local supermarket or specialty store you'll find calasparra rice and smoked paprika in Spanish delicatessens.

The art of making a great paella is to get the base of it nice and crisp and the rest cooked through so it's moist and tender. Never, ever stir a paella, as you won't achieve a nice dark crust on the bottom if you do.

8 medium green (raw) prawns
¼ cup olive oil
2 chorizo sausages, sliced
2 boneless chicken thigh fillets
    (about 140 g each), each cut into 6 slices
1 small onion, finely sliced
2 cloves garlic, finely chopped
1½ cups calasparra rice
2 teaspoons smoked paprika
½ cup peas
pinch saffron, dissolved in a little hot water
300–400 ml homemade chicken stock
    or 200 ml ready-made chicken stock
    diluted with 200 ml water
sea salt, to taste
12 cherry tomatoes, cut in half
12 mussels, 'beards' removed,
    any open shells discarded
12 fresh calamari rings
2 tablespoons chopped flat-leaf parsley
2 tablespoons chopped coriander

To prepare the prawns, twist off the head and, with a sharp knife, make a 5 mm-deep cut through the back of the shell. Pull out the dark intestinal vein and peel off the shell, leaving on the last section of tail if desired.

Heat the oil in a paella pan and add the chorizo, chicken, onion and garlic. Cook over high heat to lightly brown the chicken and the onion. Add the rice, paprika, peas and saffron mixture and stir to coat, then add half the stock. Add some sea salt (not too much if using ready-made stock). Cook the rice over low–medium heat for 10 minutes. Check and add more stock if necessary, then arrange the tomatoes and seafood over the top of the paella and continue to cook until the rice is al dente (about 10 minutes more). If any of the mussels haven't opened, place a lid over the pan for 30 seconds or so to steam them open.

Scatter over the parsley and coriander and serve.

Serves 4–6

Blackened blue eye fillets

Blackened fish is a technique done badly all over the world, even sometimes in its native New Orleans. If successful, it is a spicy, slightly smoky enhancement of a good piece of fish. If not, it just tastes burnt.

The trick is to make sure your fish fillets aren't too thick (2 cm tops), otherwise the outside will burn before the inside has a chance to cook. To really impress your guests you can try this recipe using a plate-sized whole fish like snapper – again, just make sure it's not too thick.

4 × 150 g blue eye fillets, skin on
2 tablespoons neutral oil (see page 10)
lime halves, to garnish

SPICE RUB
1 teaspoon sea salt
1½ teaspoons dried thyme
1 teaspoon dried oregano
1 teaspoon onion powder
½ teaspoon garlic powder
1 teaspoon freshly ground black pepper
½ teaspoon cayenne pepper

Mix the spice rub ingredients together and sprinkle over both sides of the fish.

Preheat a flat grillplate to very hot and pour on the oil, immediately placing the fish skin-side down as the oil sizzles. Cook for a couple of minutes on each side, sprinkling any leftover spice rub over the uncooked side of the fish before turning.

Once cooked, the fish should look, well, blackened. It should not actually be burnt, but the spices will blacken in the hot oil and give a burnt appearance. Garnish with lime halves and serve with some crusty bread.

Serves 4

Seared salmon and potato salad with grain mustard dressing

Here's something a bit different for a lunchtime one-dish salad. You can sort out the salad ingredients beforehand in the kitchen, then sear the salmon, let it rest while you whip the top off a nice bottle of crisp white wine, and then fold the fish through the salad to serve – you beauty!

8 small new potatoes
24 fresh green beans
600 g salmon fillets, skin on and pin bones removed
16 ripe cherry or grape tomatoes, cut in half

GRAIN MUSTARD DRESSING
⅓ cup olive oil
2 tablespoons white wine vinegar
1 tablespoon grain mustard
¼ cup finely chopped dill
sea salt and freshly ground black pepper, to taste

Steam or boil the potatoes until just cooked, then cut in half and reserve. Steam or boil the green beans and refresh in cold (preferably iced) water to maintain their colour and stop them cooking further.

Preheat your flat grillplate and cook the salmon, skin-side down first, for about 2 minutes each side (it should still be very rare). Remove the salmon from the grill and set aside to rest in a warm place, loosely covered with foil, for 15 minutes. It will continue to cook while resting.

Mix the dressing ingredients together in a large shallow serving bowl. Add the tomatoes, potatoes and green beans and mix through.

Remove the skin from the salmon and break the fish into large chunks, gently mixing it in with the vegetables and the dressing. Serve immediately.

Serves 4

Asian-style fish-in-a-parcel

The idea behind this wonderfully simple dish is that by cooking the fish with other ingredients inside a tightly-sealed foil parcel, it becomes infused with delicious flavours as it cooks.

Instead of a large whole fish, you could use 4 small ones or 4 × 150 g blue eye fillets, wrapping each in a foil parcel and dividing the oil, paste and lime leaves evenly between each parcel.

2 stalks lemongrass
2 knobs ginger (3 cm long), peeled
  and roughly chopped
1 clove garlic, roughly chopped
2 red shallots, peeled and sliced
1 medium red chilli, de-seeded and sliced
1 teaspoon grated palm sugar
1 tablespoon fish sauce
⅔ cup coconut cream
1 whole large snapper
1 tablespoon vegetable or peanut oil
8 kaffir lime leaves

Using a mortar and pestle or a food processor, make a paste from the lemongrass, ginger, garlic, red shallots, chilli and palm sugar. Stir through the fish sauce and coconut cream.

Make a couple of slashes with a knife on either side of the fish, taking care not to cut right through to the bone (this helps to cook the fish more evenly). Tear off one large sheet of extra-wide foil big enough to wrap the fish, and place it shiny-side up on a work surface. Spread the oil and half the paste evenly over the sheet of foil. Place the fish on top and spread the remaining paste evenly over the fish. Scatter the lime leaves on top and fold the foil up at the edges to seal.

Place the fish on a preheated flat grillplate and cook for 10 minutes, or until cooked through. Serve with boiled or steamed rice, Asian green vegetables and oyster sauce or a little sesame oil.

Serves 4

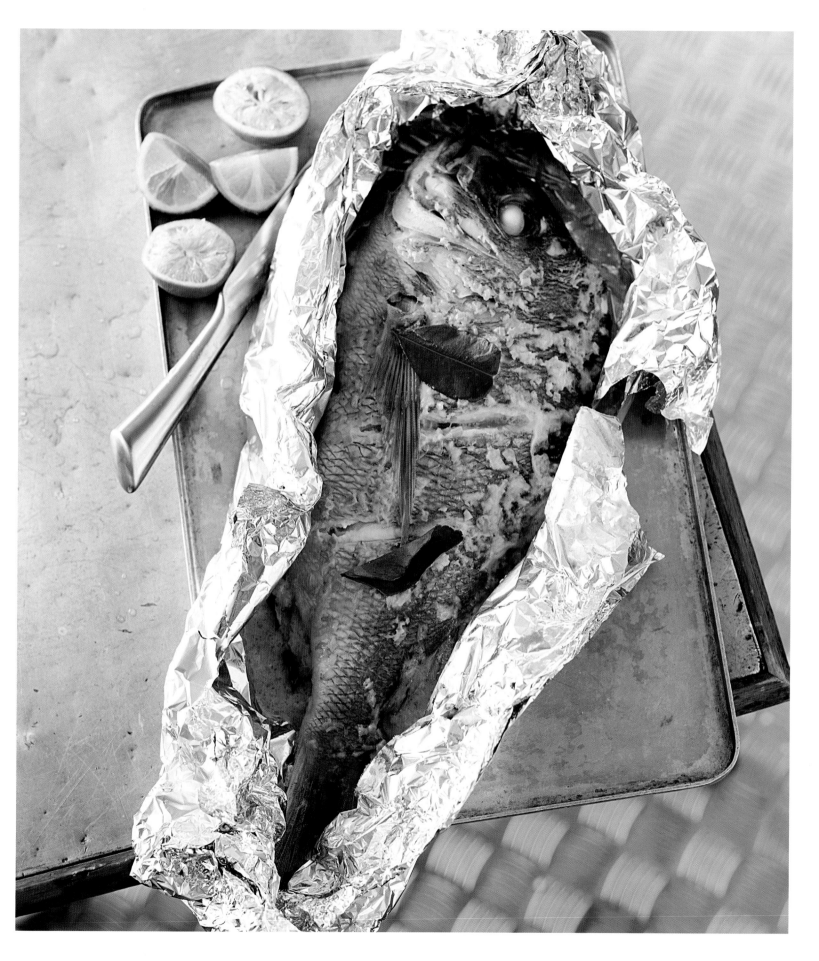

Blue eye with fennel butter

You can use any firm white fish for this. Blue eye is good because it won't fall apart on your hotplate, and the bones are big and easy to find. Ling and reef fish like coral trout also work well.

This recipe makes enough fennel butter for 4–6 serves, but you could easily make twice the amount and whack it in the freezer to smarten up your school-night barbecues.

2 tablespoons olive oil
4 × 150 g blue eye fillets, skin on

FENNEL BUTTER
1 clove garlic
2 teaspoons fennel seeds
100 g softened butter
1 teaspoon lemon juice
½ teaspoon sea salt

To make the fennel butter, firstly peel the garlic clove, soften in boiling water for 2 minutes, then crush or finely chop. Crush the fennel seeds using a mortar and pestle or spice grinder.

Combine all the fennel butter ingredients together in a small bowl and mash with the back of a fork to mix thoroughly. Transfer to a sheet of greaseproof paper, and roll into a sausage shape about the diameter of a 20-cent piece. Twist both ends to seal, then refrigerate and cut into discs as required. (It should keep for about a week in the fridge or for several months in the freezer – wrap in a layer of plastic film before freezing.)

Rub the oil over the fish and cook on a preheated flat grillplate, turning once, until just cooked through. Serve immediately with fresh salad leaves, topping each piece of fish with a disc of fennel butter.

Serves 4

Whisky and maple-glazed salmon

This is a simple and quite delicately flavoured fish dish. The real upside of this is that you will have leftover maple syrup in the fridge for pancakes, and nearly a whole bottle of Scotch hanging around and nothing to use it for . . .

4 × 150 g salmon fillets

GLAZE
¼ cup Scotch whisky
¼ cup real maple syrup
1 clove garlic, crushed
1 tablespoon neutral oil (see page 10)

Mix the glaze ingredients together in a shallow dish, then add the salmon, making sure it is well coated in the glaze. Cover with plastic film and marinate in the fridge for 2–4 hours. Bring the salmon to room temperature by removing from the fridge half an hour before cooking.

Place the salmon, skin-side down, on a preheated chargrill, and cook for about 2 minutes each side, turning once. The centre should remain very pink.

Remove the fish from the grill and set aside to rest, loosely covered with foil, for 5–10 minutes before serving with Classic Potato Salad on page 142.

Serves 4

Salad days

Classic rice salad

There's something quite Christmassy about a rice salad with ham and prawns, but it's too good to have just once a year. Here's a tip: make much more than you will need, and you will be really grateful the morning after as you forage through the fridge with a nasty hangover, looking for something – anything – to eat.

2 cups long-grain rice
½ cup cashew nuts
1 small red capsicum, white insides
 and seeds removed, finely diced
1 small green capsicum, white insides
 and seeds removed, finely diced
3 spring onions (white and pale green
 parts only), finely sliced
2 slices leg ham, finely diced
4 button mushrooms, chopped
½ cup flat-leaf parsley leaves, chopped
½ cup coriander leaves, chopped
½ cup small cooked prawns
 ***or* 2 large cooked prawns, chopped**

DRESSING
½ cup peanut oil
¼ cup white wine vinegar
1 teaspoon sea salt
freshly ground black pepper, to taste

Bring plenty of salted water to the boil in a large saucepan, then add the rice and simmer, uncovered, for about 10 minutes or until cooked. Drain and rinse under cold water in a colander or sieve, and set aside to cool.

Lightly toast the cashew nuts in a dry non-stick frying pan for a couple of minutes until browned, then set aside to cool. (Be careful – they can go from golden brown to burnt in a matter of seconds.)

Mix the dressing ingredients together.

Combine the cooked rice, toasted cashews and the rest of the ingredients in a large bowl, stir through the dressing and serve.

Serves 4–6 as a side dish

Caprese salad

The secret to this very simple dish is the top-quality ingredients. It just won't work with unripe, flavourless tomatoes, 'plastic' pizza mozzarella and a crook olive oil.

Cut the mozzarella into neat slices if you like, or you can tear it apart with your fingers – it tastes just as good.

4 ripe tomatoes, oxhearts if you can find them
300–400 g fresh mozzarella or imported buffalo mozzarella
sea salt and freshly ground black pepper, to taste
about 16 fresh basil leaves
extra virgin olive oil, to drizzle

Cut the tomatoes and mozzarella into slices of equal thickness (about 7 mm thick). On serving plates, arrange alternate layers of tomato slices and mozzarella slices. Season well with salt and pepper, top with the basil leaves and drizzle plenty of olive oil over the lot.

Serves 4 as a light entrée or 6 as a side dish

Caprese salad

Baked beetroot and pumpkin salad

This salad is a showcase for just how good fresh beetroot tastes. Do not even consider the canned stuff as a substitute in this dish, because while it's mandatory in a hamburger, it's not right for a stylish salad like this. It's horses for courses, you see.

400 g pumpkin, cut into 4 cm chunks

olive oil, for coating

sea salt and freshly ground black pepper, to taste

9 baby beetroot, tops trimmed,
   tender inner leaves washed and reserved

50 g butter

½ cup walnuts

⅓ cup extra virgin olive oil

2 tablespoons good-quality balsamic vinegar

1 stick celery, sliced

200 g goat's curd or mild soft goat's cheese

2 tablespoons finely chopped dill

Preheat the oven to 180°C.

Lightly coat the pumpkin pieces in oil and season with salt and pepper, then roast until tender – about 30–40 minutes.

Wrap each beetroot, with half a teaspoon of the butter and a little salt and pepper, in foil and roast on a baking tray in the oven for about 30 minutes, or until tender. When the beetroot is cool enough to handle, remove the remaining stalks and rub the skins off with your fingers (use thin plastic disposable gloves to protect your hands), then cut each beetroot into quarters or halves.

Lightly toast the walnuts in a dry non-stick frying pan for a couple of minutes until browned, then set aside to cool.

Make the dressing in a bowl by mixing the oil and vinegar with some salt and pepper. Add the pumpkin, beetroot, washed beetroot leaves and celery, and toss gently.

Crumble the cheese or curd over the salad, sprinkle with dill and serve.

Serves 4 as a light entrée or 6 as a side dish

Asian rice salad

The ingredients used here are pretty much the same as for your standard Chinese take-away fried rice, except this dish is served cold. Like traditional fried rice, you boil the rice in lots of water and then drain it, rather than steaming it, so the grains separate instead of sticking together. You can buy char siu in your local Chinese food store or at Chinatown.

2 cups long-grain rice
3 eggs
neutral oil (see page 10), for frying
1 bunch gai lan (Chinese broccoli),
**   trimmed and chopped**
⅔ cup small cooked prawns *or* 3 large
**   cooked prawns, chopped**
1 small piece char siu (Chinese
**   barbecued pork), finely chopped**
4 spring onions, finely sliced
1 tablespoon light soy sauce
2 tablespoons mirin
2 tablespoons peanut oil
1 teaspoon sesame oil
1 cup coriander leaves

Bring plenty of salted water to the boil in a large saucepan, then add the rice and simmer, uncovered, for about 10 minutes or until cooked. Drain and rinse under cold water in a sieve, and set aside to cool.

In a bowl, beat the eggs lightly with a fork, then heat a small amount of neutral oil in a non-stick frying pan and pour in the egg mixture, tipping the pan from side to side so it spreads out evenly. Cook for a couple of minutes, tipping the pan again from time to time to allow the uncooked egg to move to the edges. Once cooked, remove the omelette from the pan and set aside to cool, then finely dice.

Blanch the gai lan in freshly boiled water for 30 seconds, then remove and refresh immediately in cold water.

Combine the cooled rice, omelette pieces and gai lan with the remaining ingredients in a large salad bowl, and serve chilled.

Serves 6 as a side dish

Tomato and onion salad

A classic, simple salad like this is the perfect accompaniment to barbecued meat. You can use any variety of tomato as long as they're fresh – the quality of the tomatoes will make or break this dish.

3 very ripe tomatoes, thickly sliced
1 small red onion, thinly sliced
1 tablespoon torn basil or flat-leaf parsley leaves
½ cup small black olives, preferably Ligurian

DRESSING
⅓ cup extra virgin olive oil
2 tablespoons balsamic vinegar
sea salt and freshly ground black pepper, to taste

Mix the dressing ingredients together and reserve.

Place the tomatoes, onions, basil or parsley and olives in a large salad bowl, spoon the dressing over the top and serve immediately.

Serves 4 as a side dish

Classic potato salad

Astonish yourself and make your own mayonnaise for this simple potato salad – it's much easier than you think. You might need an assistant to act as the oil-drizzler.

You can either use new potatoes, and leave the skins on, or any waxy yellow variety like kipfler, but these will need peeling.

750 g small new potatoes
2 eggs
1 bunch chives, finely chopped
sea salt and freshly ground black pepper, to taste

HOMEMADE MAYONNAISE
2 egg yolks
½ teaspoon Dijon mustard
about 1 cup olive oil
sea salt, to taste
lemon juice, to taste

Bring a large saucepan of salted water to the boil and cook the potatoes for about 10–15 minutes, or until tender. Drain immediately and allow to cool, then cut into 2 cm chunks.

In a small saucepan, boil some water, then add the eggs and cook for 5 minutes. Rinse immediately under cold water, and set aside. Once the eggs have cooled, peel and slice them.

To make the mayonnaise, place the egg yolks and Dijon mustard in a large bowl. Add the olive oil in a fine drizzle while whisking vigorously with a wire whisk or a fork until the mixture thickens. (You can cheat and use an electric mixer if you must.) Season with a little sea salt and add a few drops of lemon juice.

Gently combine the potato, egg and mayonnaise together in a serving bowl, sprinkle over the chives and season with salt and pepper.

Serves 6

Broad bean
and corn relish

Broad bean and corn relish

This is sort of a relish, sort of a salad. Either way, it is a fine partner to a nice piece of veal or grilled fish. You'll probably find that it's a bit too sweet to pair with lamb or beef.

2 corn cobs
1 kg broad beans, shelled
2 tablespoons cream
2 tablespoons lemon juice
6 mint leaves, finely sliced
sea salt and freshly ground black pepper, to taste

Bring a large saucepan of water to the boil, add the corn cobs and cook, covered, for 10–15 minutes or until tender.

In a small saucepan, bring some water to the boil, then add the broad beans and cook for 30 seconds. Drain and allow to cool for a few minutes, then remove the tough outer skins.

Once the corn is cool enough to handle, stand each cob on its side on a chopping board and carefully slice the kernels off with a large knife.

Combine the corn kernels and broad beans with the remaining ingredients in a bowl and serve.

Serves 4 as a side dish

Classic coleslaw

Here's a basic coleslaw recipe to which you can add anything that takes your fancy. Sultanas, lemon juice and plenty of grain mustard is a particularly nice variation.

If you're feeling especially brave, you could make your own mayonnaise instead of using a ready-made one – see the recipe on page 142.

2 carrots, peeled and grated
2 sticks celery, finely sliced
¼ white cabbage (thick white stems removed),
    very finely sliced
1 small red onion, very finely sliced
½ cup finely chopped flat-leaf parsley
1 cup ready-made coleslaw dressing or mayonnaise
sea salt, to taste

Mix all the ingredients together in a large bowl. Cover the coleslaw and chill in the fridge for half an hour before serving.

Serves 4–6 as a side dish

Tomato rice salad

This dish is designed as an accompaniment, but can become the main attraction with the addition of either some chopped ham, cooked prawns, cooked and shredded chicken breast or sliced and lightly sautéed button mushrooms.

500 g long-grain rice
½ cup slivered almonds
2 cloves garlic, crushed
1 medium brown onion, finely diced
1 tablespoon olive oil
2 × 400 g cans chopped tomatoes
1 heaped tablespoon tomato paste
½ cup chopped flat-leaf parsley
½ cup shredded basil leaves
2 tablespoons extra virgin olive oil
1 tablespoon balsamic vinegar
sea salt and black pepper, to taste

Bring plenty of salted water to the boil in a large saucepan, then add the rice and simmer, uncovered, for about 10 minutes or until cooked. Drain and rinse under cold water in a colander or sieve, and set aside to cool.

While the rice is cooking, lightly toast the slivered almonds in a dry non-stick frying pan for a couple of minutes until browned, then set aside to cool.

Soften the garlic and onion in the olive oil in a large frying pan. Add the tomatoes and tomato paste and simmer for 10 minutes. Remove from the heat, add the cooked rice and allow to cool.

To serve, stir through the fresh herbs, toasted almonds, extra virgin olive oil and balsamic vinegar, and season with salt and pepper.

Serves 6–8 as a side dish

Pasta, pine nut and fresh herb salad

Pasta and pine nuts go so well together that it makes sense to combine them in a salad. Keep an eye on the pine nuts when toasting them though – they can go from golden brown to burnt in a matter of seconds.

1 cup orecchiette, orzo or similar
    small pasta shapes
½ cup pine nuts
1 tablespoon chopped chives
1 tablespoon chopped flat-leaf parsley
1 tablespoon finely sliced basil leaves

DRESSING
¼ cup extra virgin olive oil
2 tablespoons white wine vinegar
½ clove garlic, crushed
sea salt and freshly ground black pepper, to taste

Bring plenty of salted water to the boil in a large saucepan, then add the pasta and simmer until al dente. Drain and rinse under cold water in a colander or sieve, and set aside to cool.

Lightly toast the pine nuts in a dry non-stick frying pan for a couple of minutes until browned, then set aside to cool.

Mix the dressing ingredients together in the base of a large salad bowl, and then toss all the other ingredients together, mixing the dressing through. Serve immediately.

Serves 4 as a side dish

Pasta, pine nut and
fresh herb salad

Hawaiian macaroni salad

There is something about this dish that brings to mind *Women's Weekly* recipes, circa 1960. To make it a little less naff, you can lose the pineapple if you like.

2½ cups (400 g) macaroni-shaped pasta
6 eggs
⅔ cup canned crushed pineapple
2 spring onions (white part only), finely sliced
1 stick celery, finely sliced
1–1½ cups ready-made mayonnaise
1 teaspoon paprika
sea salt and freshly ground black pepper, to taste

Bring plenty of salted water to the boil in a large saucepan, then add the pasta and simmer until al dente. Drain and rinse under cold water in a colander or sieve, and set aside to cool.

In a small saucepan, boil some water, then add the eggs and cook for 5 minutes. Rinse immediately under cold water, and set aside. Once the eggs have cooled, peel and finely chop them.

Combine the cooked pasta and egg with the rest of the ingredients in a salad bowl and serve.

Serves 6 as a side dish

Sugar snap pea and walnut salad

What could be simpler than this crunchy little number? Make sure that your sugar snap peas are firm and green, and that your tomatoes are not.

2 cups sugar snap peas, ends trimmed
2 tablespoons walnut oil
1 tablespoon extra virgin olive oil
1 tablespoon lemon juice
sea salt and freshly ground black pepper, to taste
⅔ cup walnut halves
8 ripe cherry tomatoes, cut in half

Blanch the peas by plunging them into a saucepan of salted boiling water for 30 seconds. Drain them and refresh by placing immediately in a bowl of iced water. When they have cooled completely, drain well and set aside.

Mix the oils with the lemon juice, salt and pepper in a large serving bowl, then stir through the peas and the rest of the ingredients and serve immediately.

Serves 4 as a side dish

Sugar snap pea
and walnut salad

Spring salad

The variations on this are endless – you can throw almost any fresh, green vegetables in, and dress it with any good-quality oil and vinegar.

Fresh goat's curd is a mild goat's cheese that adds something really special to salads, and you'll find it in specialty delis or cheese shops.

2 bunches asparagus, ends trimmed,
 cut into 3 cm pieces
2 cups broccoli florets
2 cups sugar snap peas
1 cup shelled broad beans
½ cup toasted walnuts
about 10 sage leaves
½ cup walnut oil
⅓ cup white wine vinegar
sea salt and freshly ground black pepper, to taste
1 cup fresh goat's curd

Steam the asparagus, broccoli and sugar snap peas together in a steamer over boiling water for a minute or two, until just cooked but still firm. Alternatively, you can blanch them by plunging them into a saucepan of salted boiling water for about 30 seconds, then draining them. Refresh the vegetables by placing immediately in a bowl of iced water (this stops them cooking and keeps them nice and green).

In a small saucepan, bring some water to the boil and add the broad beans, cooking for about 30 seconds. Drain and allow them to cool for a few minutes, then remove the tough outer skins and set aside.

Lightly toast the walnuts in a dry non-stick frying pan for a couple of minutes until browned, then set aside to cool. (Be careful – they can go from golden brown to burnt in a matter of seconds.) Heat a little olive oil in the pan and lightly fry the sage leaves until just crisp.

Make the dressing in your serving bowl by mixing the walnut oil, vinegar, salt and pepper. Add the asparagus, broccoli, peas and broad beans and toss to coat well in the dressing. Spoon over the sage leaves and nuts, and crumble the goat's curd on top.

Serves 4 as an entrée or 6 as a side dish

Wild rice salad

Wild rice isn't rice at all. In fact it comes from a type of grass that grows taller than a West Indian fast bowler. It takes quite a while to cook but has miles more flavour and texture than ordinary rice, and makes a very different sort of rice salad.

½ cup currants
2 tablespoons white wine
1 cup wild rice
1 corn cob
½ cup pine nuts
½ cup slivered almonds
½ cup extra virgin olive oil
⅓ cup white wine vinegar
sea salt and freshly ground black pepper, to taste
2 spring onions (white and pale green
    parts only), finely sliced
1 small green capsicum, white insides
    and seeds removed, diced
1 small red capsicum, white insides
    and seeds removed, diced
1 cup coriander leaves

Soak the currants in the white wine for 30 minutes, then drain, discarding the wine, and set aside.

Bring the rice and 3 cups of water to the boil in a saucepan, then turn the heat down and simmer, covered, until the rice is cooked (this should take about 40 minutes). Drain and set aside to cool.

Bring a large saucepan of water to the boil, add the corn and cover, cooking for 10–15 minutes, or until tender.

Lightly toast the pine nuts and almonds in a dry non-stick frying pan for a couple of minutes until browned. Keep a close eye on them, as they'll burn in a heartbeat.

Once the corn is cool enough to handle, stand the cob on its side on a chopping board and carefully slice the kernels off with a large knife.

Combine the oil with the vinegar, salt and pepper in the base of a large salad bowl. Mix the rice, currants, nuts and all the other ingredients through the dressing, and serve.

Serves 6–8 as a side dish

Something sweet

BBQ fruit salad
with rum

Ok, so this is the ultimate daggy dessert – but try telling your guests that as they come back for more. If you're having a family barbecue, don't worry about the rum and kids combination – the alcohol will evaporate on cooking, leaving a nice edge to the sauce.

2 tablespoons sultanas
½ cup Bundaberg rum
100 g unsalted butter
½ ripe pineapple, peeled and cut into 2–3 cm chunks
3 oranges, peeled and segmented
3 bananas, peeled and thickly sliced
18 strawberries, cut in half if large
2 tablespoons brown sugar
2 teaspoons ground cinnamon (optional)

Soak the sultanas in the rum for half an hour.

Heat your roasting dish or wok over a high heat, and add the butter, stirring frequently so it doesn't brown. Add the fruit and stir gently until the fruit is warmed through.

Add the brown sugar and cinnamon, if using, and stir through until the sugar dissolves. Stir in the sultanas and rum, and cook for 30 seconds or so until the alcohol has evaporated. Serve the warm fruit salad in individual bowls, each topped with a scoop of ice cream.

Serves 6

Caramelised mangoes with coconut sauce

Thai-style desserts can seem a bit intimidating, but simply dissolving palm sugar in coconut cream creates an amazingly rich sauce to serve with mangoes or other tropical fruit. Palm sugar is available in some large supermarkets with special Asian sections, or in any Asian food store.

1 cup coconut milk
½ cup grated palm sugar
4 mangoes, cheeks cut close to the stone
4 tablespoons castor sugar

Place the coconut milk in a small saucepan and add the palm sugar, cooking over a low heat until all the sugar has dissolved. Transfer to a small bowl, cover and place in the fridge to cool.

Sprinkle the castor sugar evenly over the cut sides of the mango cheeks. Preheat your chargrill to very hot.

Place each mango cheek cut-side down on the hot chargrill, and cook for 1–2 minutes until the sugar has caramelised – the fruit only needs to warm through.

Remove the mangoes from the grill and place two on each plate, cut-side up, and leave to rest for a minute to allow the sugar to harden to a thin toffee. Spoon over some cooled coconut sauce and serve.

Serves 4

Grilled pineapple with pecan nuts and caramel sauce

This recipe may sound a bit fiddly, but it's actually very quick because you are cooking three things at once. All you need are two more pairs of hands.

1 ripe pineapple, peeled and cut
   into eight 1.5 cm slices
2 tablespoons vegetable oil
1 cup shelled pecan nuts

CARAMEL SAUCE
1 cup sugar
2 tablespoons water
1 cup cream

To make the sauce, heat the sugar and water in a wok or saucepan and stir through until the sugar has dissolved. Continue to cook until the sugar has turned a golden brown (don't let it get too dark), and then pour in the cream. Be careful here as the hot mixture may sizzle and spit as you do this. Turn the heat down to low and simmer for a minute or two.

In the meantime, brush the pineapple slices with oil and cook over a high heat on the chargrill for a couple of minutes each side. At the same time, toast the pecans on the flat grillplate over medium heat for a minute or two – keep a close eye on them as they'll burn in a heartbeat.

To serve, place two slices of pineapple on each plate and spoon over some caramel sauce. Scatter the pecans over the top and serve with thickened cream or ice cream.

Serves 4

Grilled freestone peaches with raspberry sauce and pistachios

You only have a short window after Christmas to make these, because not only do you have to use fresh peaches, but they must be freestones; they're the ones where the fruit just pulls away from the stone. If you don't know why you have to use freestones, just try cutting a regular peach in half and removing the stone – it gets messy.

4 freestone peaches, peeled and cut in half
2 tablespoons vegetable oil
½ teaspoon grated nutmeg
⅔ cup peeled pistachio nuts, lightly crushed

RASPBERRY SAUCE
200 g raspberries (frozen are fine)
2 tablespoons castor sugar
1 teaspoon lemon juice
2 tablespoons water

If using frozen raspberries, take them out of the freezer to defrost about 15 minutes before use.

Place all the sauce ingredients in a food processor or blender and process to a thin pouring consistency.

Brush the peach halves with the oil and sprinkle a pinch of the nutmeg over the inside of the peaches. Place the peaches on a very hot chargrill, cut-side down first, and cook for about a minute and a half on each side.

Serve two peach halves on each plate and spoon over the raspberry sauce. Top with the crushed pistachios.

Serves 4

Hot banana split with chocolate sauce

To avoid your bananas going mushy, the trick here is to grill them really quickly over a very high heat – a preheated grillplate is the way to go.

You can use a ready-made chocolate sauce and serve it cold or warmed in the microwave, but there's something special about making one from scratch.

**4 large bananas, peeled and cut
  in half lengthways**
2 tablespoons melted butter
4 scoops each vanilla and chocolate ice cream
**1 cup marshmallows, cut into quarters
  or 1 cup small marshmallows**
⅓ cup unsalted crushed nuts

CHOCOLATE SAUCE
**100 g good-quality dark chocolate,
  broken into pieces**
1 cup cream

To make the chocolate sauce, melt the chocolate and cream over a very low heat in a small saucepan.

Brush the bananas with the melted butter and cook on a very hot chargrill for about 30 seconds each side.

Place two pieces of banana in each bowl and top with a scoop of vanilla and chocolate ice cream. Scatter marshmallows over and pour the chocolate sauce over the top. Sprinkle with some crushed nuts and serve immediately.

Serves 4

Mangoes with chilli and lime

You know summer is here when mangoes hit the shops – is there a better smell than that of a deliciously ripe mango? They're the perfect fruit to eat on their own, but this recipe will add some Asian zestiness to your dessert.

4 tablespoons castor sugar
1 tablespoon grated palm sugar
4 teaspoons very finely chopped and
    de-seeded medium red chilli
4 teaspoons very finely grated lime zest
4 mangoes, cheeks cut close to the stone
lime wedges, to garnish

Mix the sugars, chilli and lime zest together and sprinkle over the cut sides of the mango cheeks.

Place the mango cheeks cut-side down on a very hot flat grillplate, and cook just until the sugar turns dark brown and starts to crisp, being careful not to let it burn.

Serve immediately, garnished with lime wedges.

Serves 4

Toasted brioche with butterscotch strawberries

This is a nice, luxurious treat, and only takes a minute or two to make, but beware – a real sweet tooth is required. You can buy brioche from most bakeries and patisseries.

50 g butter
2 punnets ripe strawberries,
    washed and green tops removed
150 g brown sugar
1 cup cream
4 slices brioche (about 2 cm thick)

In a wok or saucepan over medium heat, melt the butter, then add the strawberries and cook for about 30 seconds before adding the brown sugar. Once the sugar has dissolved, pour in the cream and simmer for 1 minute. Make sure you don't overcook the mixture – the strawberries should be soft but remain whole.

Meanwhile, grill the brioche on both sides on a chargrill over high heat until the outside is lightly toasted.

Place a slice of brioche on each plate and spoon over the strawberry and butterscotch sauce. Serve with ice cream or thickened cream, if desired.

Serves 4

Toasted brioche with
butterscotch strawberries

Cheers...

This is my first book and it would not have been possible without the help of some very talented people.

Rob Palmer makes food look great and shooting it a very calm process. David Morgan brought a sense of style to the shots that I certainly don't have.

'The girls' at Penguin, Julie Gibbs, Ingrid Ohlsson and Virginia Birch have each forgotten more than I will ever know about publishing a book and stopped me from translating my over-the-top blokey-ness and dagginess to the pages. Thanks also to Daniel New for making the design so clean, smart and user-friendly.

I have to thank my aussiebarbie.com.au sponsors, without whom this book and the entire aussiebarbie activity would not be possible. Meat & Livestock Australia, MasterFoods, Swap'n'Go, Everdure and Sunbeam have all been great supporters over the past year and a half.

Kim Terakes' twenty-five-year advertising career was really just an excuse to have lunch in restaurants every day. He has since given up the pretence and now devotes himself exclusively to the cause of good food. Since the late 1980s, he has written about food and restaurants for publications such as *Australian Gourmet Traveller*, *Vogue Entertaining*, *BRW*, *SMH Good Living* and the *Sunday Telegraph*. He was the restaurant reviewer for the *Sun-Herald* for several years, and contributed to the *Good Food Guide* throughout the 1990s. He has been the food writer for *GQ* magazine for the past five years.

Kim started the Boys Can Cook cooking school (boyscancook.com.au) in 2004 and also runs aussiebarbie.com.au. He is passionate about teaching Aussie blokes how to be useful in the kitchen and inspirational at the barbecue.

Index